To John
With Appreciation for
Another fan of LA History
and The Chandler Story

Bill Boyarsky

Inventing L.A.
LOST ANGELES

ACP

ANGEL CITY PRESS

Inventing L.A.

DESTINY

"Sail on! sail on! sail on! and on!"

LOS ANGELES

GREATER SOUTHERN CALIFORNIA
STRAIGHT AHEAD

FIRST EDITION

Liberty Under Law—Equal Rights—True Industrial Freedom.

Inventing L.A.: The Chandlers and Their Times

BY BILL BOYARSKY | BASED ON THE FILM BY PETER JONES

PHOTOGRAPHY EDITORS: MARK CATALENA AND BRIAN TESSIER | DESIGN: AMY INOUYE

A DYNASTY, A CITY

PIONEER: *Harrison Gray Otis took over the young paper.*

BUILDER: *Harry Chandler amassed vast land holdings.*

ANOINTER: *Norman Chandler wielded GOP power.*

PATRON: *Dorothy Chandler led the Music Center effort.*

TRANSFORMER: *Otis Chandler remade The Times.*

Empire's Saga Embroidered by Myth

[History, from Page A1]

ers, speculators and goatherds; a long run of clubby white capitalists, who, one generation removed from their goats, liked to think of themselves as "old money"; a latter-day installment of corporate elites, whose moment was crowned with the 1984 Olympics they sponsored; and, finally, a splintering off into many pieces.

Those who study Los Angeles today employ terms like "horizontal" and "diffuse" to describe the city's power structure. They talk of a power vacuum and note that, with so many of its old Fortune 500 companies dissolved, bought up, relocated, Los Angeles has become something of a "branch city." Whether this represents a good or bad development is open to interpretation.

"Today there is no single node of power in the city," said Mayor Antonio Villaraigosa. "It's diffused geographically, diffused among important stakeholders — business, labor, for instance — and also racially and ethnically.... There is a devolution of power today that is more grass-roots and more focused on specific neighborhoods."

Indeed, if the skyscrapers of downtown symbolized a certain era of influence in Los Angeles, so too do the small phalanxes of pro-union demonstrators who now converge beneath those gleaming towers, waving picket signs and chanting, "No justice, no peace," sometimes in Spanish, sometimes in English.

Of course, the social architecture of

Contents

8 . . . Introduction

17 . . . Chapter One . . . . . Harrison Gray Otis: The Pioneer

49 . . . Chapter Two . . . . . The Bombing

71 . . . Chapter Three . . . Harry Chandler: The Empire Builder

105 . . . Chapter Four . . . . . Norman Chandler: The Businessman

139 . . . Chapter Five . . . . . Otis Chandler: The Journalist

175 . . . Chapter Six . . . . . . Tom Johnson: The Successor

193 . . . Epilogue . . . . The Chandler Era Ends

200 . . . Acknowledgments

201 . . . Photo Credits

202 . . . Bibliography

204 . . . Index

THIS BOOK IS DEDICATED
TO THE *Los Angeles Times* JOURNALISTS WHO,
THROUGH GOOD TIMES AND BAD,
HAVE WORKED TO DELIVER THE NEWS,
ESPECIALLY TO THE PRESENT GENERATION
FACING CHALLENGES NEVER IMAGINED BY THEIR PREDECESSORS.

Introduction

When I went to work for the *Los Angeles Times* in 1970, I was first impressed by the grandly appointed lobby with its enormous globe. As time went by, I focused on other features of the Globe Lobby—busts of former publishers, General Harrison Gray Otis, Harry Chandler and Norman Chandler—that summoned up reminders of the paper's history.

The likeness of the first publisher, General Otis, made him appear fierce. From that day until I retired in 2001, I never looked at his bust without thinking how much I'd have hated to have to ask this man for a raise. His steely determination and Harry Chandler's cunning and business skill—combined with a vision they shared—helped transform L.A. from a dusty frontier town to a huge metropolis that extends far beyond the city boundaries into the vast area of the Southland. Norman made the paper into a profitable enterprise. His son, Otis, made the *Los Angeles Times* a great newspaper that was even more profitable.

Their history, and that of the Southland, was intertwined with politics. It wasn't the idealized process described in textbooks but the real-life, rough and tumble mess with plenty of conflict and intrigue, much more interesting to a political reporter like myself. It still is, which is why I accepted Angel City Press's invitation to write this book based on Peter Jones's documentary, *Inventing L.A.: The Chandlers & Their Times.*

As a reporter, I encountered constant reminders of the days when the Chandlers ran politics and government in Los Angeles and the state capital, shaping much of California's growth. For a story on Los Angeles water that my wife Nancy and I wrote for the *Los Angeles Times* magazine, we traced the water from a Los Angeles reservoir to its source in the Owens Valley, and dug into the politics, clean and dirty, that made the project possible. Over at City Hall, I sat in the council chamber in the same place where a former powerful *Times* reporter signaled council members how to vote on measures that were important to the paper. In Sacramento, veteran newsmen told me stories of how another *Times* correspondent had done the same in the state legislature. They reminisced about an even more powerful *Times* man, Kyle Palmer, the political writer who called the shots in the California Republican Party for many years.

Palmer was dead by the time I joined the *Times* staff, and Otis Chandler insisted on unbiased political reporting. To satisfy my interest in the old days, I would take a short walk from the paper to the office of retired Pacific Mutual president, the late Asa Call. Call was one of the most powerful Republicans in California from the mid-1930s to the late 1950s. With time on his hands, he seemed to enjoy talking to a reporter who was so interested in his stories. My favorite took place just after World War II. His wife attended an event in Whittier and came back impressed with a young Navy vet running for Congress. Asa checked him out, was similarly impressed, and told his friend Norman Chandler. Chandler passed the information to Palmer and that's how the political career of Richard M. Nixon began.

I had known Otis Chandler casually during most of my years at the paper. As a political writer, I was invited to his luncheons with political figures in the Norman Chandler Pavilion, the upstairs dining room named for Otis's father. Otis presided at the lunches, which were more formal than any journalistic event I had attended in the working-class culture of my previous employers, the Associated Press and the *Oakland Tribune*. The questions were always polite. There were periods of silence, made noticeable by the clanking of the expensive silverware. Everyone ate slowly, chewing their food and drinking their non-alcoholic beverage thoughtfully. I learned to lower my voice, refrain from the press conference mentality, and word my questions tactfully. Mostly, I listened and learned and came away thinking Otis was a smart, decent, and well-informed man.

Toward the end of my *Times* career, when I was city editor, he called me up one day at the paper. Incompetent management had plunged the *Times* into an ethical scandal, and Chandler, no longer with the paper, was outraged. He said he had a message he wanted me to deliver to the staff. I turned to my computer and began taking it down. It was an angry message, denouncing the paper's current management. My bosses asked me not to read it, but I felt an obligation to Chandler, who had created the great paper. So I used a staff-wide computer message to invite everyone to the third floor to hear what Otis had to say. At the appointed time, I delivered the message to a newsroom packed with my colleagues.

In the tense moments before I spoke, it also occurred to me that when I read the message, I could become a small part of the rich history of the *Times*, maybe a footnote. What history junkie could pass up a chance like that?

—BILL BOYARSKY

When Harrison and Eliza Otis arrived in Los Angeles, it was a sleepy agricultural town of 12,000 people.

The first edition of the *Times*
was published on December 4, 1881.
It had four pages and cost a penny.

The Times.
LOS ANGELES
EVERY DAY
AND
ated Sunday Magazine.
SPECIA
ITY DELIVERY.
THE TIMES

"He had this extraordinary sense that American civilization's next big phase of development would occur in the south coast of California." —Kevin Starr

"No single family has dominated any major region of the country as the Chandlers have dominated Southern California. They did not so much foster the growth of Los Angeles as invent it." —David Halberstam

CHAPTER ONE

Harrison Gray Otis: The Pioneer

The story of the Chandlers and Los Angeles began modestly in 1882 in a small print shop a mile or so south of the spot where the Spaniards first established the city. This was where Harrison Gray Otis, whose service in the Civil War had earned him the title of colonel, and his wife, Eliza, put out the *Los Angeles Daily Times*. Otis handled the hard news and editorials. Eliza, a poet, was in charge of coverage of religion, society, and culture. Theirs was the same paper that would one day be called the *Los Angeles Times*, heart of one of America's most powerful media empires. And theirs was the same family that would one day, through the marriage of their daughter, become The Chandlers.

Three generations of the family dynasty gather for the annual Chandler Christmas party, 1930. Patriarch Harry Chandler is at far right with his wife Marian to his right. Harry's son Norman (face partly obscured), fourth from left in back row, holding his son, Otis. In front of them is Norman's wife Dorothy with her arms around their daughter, Camilla. PAGES 10-11: View of Los Angeles in its early days, long before development booms.
PAGES 12-13: A *Times* delivery truck arrives at the train station, where a group of civic-minded Angelenos have gathered at the turn of the century.
PAGE 14: As publisher of the *Times*, General Otis was often posed with well-wishers. PAGE 15: General Otis (facing backward in carriage) in Pasadena's Rose Parade circa 1895.

Colonel Otis—he later worked his way up to general in the Spanish-American War—along with a small number of like-minded immigrants from the Midwest and East, seized Southern California, a semi-arid desert, converted tiny Los Angeles into a huge metropolis, and became rich. Although staunch believers in private enterprise, these people saw no contradiction in furthering their own interests by using the power of government to bring water to the dry land and dig a harbor in shallow tidelands. With the arrival of water, vast acres of agricultural land—a substantial amount owned by Otis and his allies—were turned into mile after mile of residential subdivisions.

Otis saw the potential riches that could be taken from the dry landscape that extended inland from the Pacific Ocean. He was a blustery, bellicose man who approached life as if it were the Civil War battlefield of Antietam, where he had led the Twelfth Ohio Volunteers against the Confederates in the bloodiest one-day battle in American history. "The enemy's rear has been fiercely shelled by us, & he no doubt returns to Virginia with shattered columns," he wrote a few days after the battle. It was the kind of punishment he would wish on his enemies for the rest of his life.

His many enemies responded in kind. One of them, California's early twentieth-century reform governor, Hiram Johnson, said of Otis:

> He sits there in senile dementia, with gangrened heart and rotting brain, grimacing at every reform, chattering impotently at all things that are decent, frothing, fuming, violently gibbering, going down to his grave in snarling infamy. This man Otis is the one blot on the banner of Southern California; he is the bar sinister on your escutcheon. My friends, he is the one thing that all California looks at, when, in looking at Southern California, they see anything that is disgraceful, depraved, corrupt, crooked and putrescent—that is Harrison Gray Otis.

Despite his detractors, Otis and his business prospered as one land boom followed another, along with an oil boom. In 1892, thirty-six-year-old Edward L. Doheny, an unsuccessful mining prospector, struck oil in a residential area west of downtown Los Angeles, setting off a rush for oil. "Actually," wrote Carey McWilliams, "the growth of Southern California since 1870 should be regarded as one continuous boom punctuated at intervals by major explosions."

On June 25, 1861, Harrison Gray Otis enlisted as a private in the Infantry. By the time he was mustered out, he had been promoted to lieutenant colonel.

FRONTIER EDITOR

When Otis began his career in Ohio, men like him were familiar figures in the West: the frontier editor. Like the others, he'd learned the trade in a print shop. As publisher, editor, reporter, and printer—often one person performed all these functions—he walked unpaved streets in search of news items and advertisements and wrote stories he hoped would lure visitors, prospective residents, and advertisers to his dusty town.

Otis was born in a small Ohio town in 1837, the youngest of sixteen children. At fourteen, he was hired as a printer's devil, an apprentice, at Ohio's *Noble County Courier*. In the frontier West, these small print shops, putting out weekly newspapers, provided a way for an intelligent, diligent country boy to break out of the limitations of rural life. One of the most famous frontier printer's devils was young Sam Clemens, who later became Mark Twain. Clemens learned to set type and run presses in small-town newspaper offices, where he also developed his taste for reading and began writing. Like Clemens, Otis trained

as a printer in several print shops. In 1856, looking to better himself, he enrolled in Wetherby's Academy in Lowell, Ohio, where he met one of the teachers, Eliza Wetherby, the daughter of the school's founder. The two fell in love. Describing the match, Ann Gordon Condon wrote in *Architects of Our Fortunes: The Journal of Eliza A.W. Otis*, "[T]he union of the cultivated Miss Wetherby with a man three and one-half years her junior, of no obvious promise, would have created quite a stir in the small town of Lowell. One can almost hear the sniffing behind the handkerchiefs of the local gossips. Yet Eliza's journal makes it clear that she found many admirable qualities in this rough-hewn young man."

Otis—she called him Harry—couldn't find a job. He wrote to her:

O, I must do a better and braver work for my wife than I have ever done in my life! It makes me almost ashamed to think that *I yield to circumstances rather than make them yield to me.* I would not have you think that I am devoid of "pluck" for I don't believe it is true. I know sometimes I evince something like a timid spirit, but you know that it is more the shrinking from certain associations than from a hard task.

Two days later, he wrote:

Dear, Darling Wife: How could I live without you! Lizzie, it would never do for me to be a missionary, a sailor, or a fisherman, or if I were to turn my attention to any of those occupations you would certainly have to prepare yourself to be a voyager along with me: I couldn't get on without my wife. Who could supply that strength, that vitality, that life-essence but my Lizzie?

Although her reply to this letter has been lost, an entry in her journal several months later reflects her own insecurities:

Every day should be a record of usefulness and every night should find us higher in our progressive life. But my advance, I fear, is somewhat snail like and not always certain at that. My life, I fear, is one of thought more than of action. There's a feeling within me as if I was not true to myself—true to my life mission. I yield too much to circumstances, and settle down into an inaction that is not life. Yet I don't believe that we need to be creatures of circumstances, but rather creators of them, and thus *architects of our own fortunes.*

Even as a young man, Otis had a thirst for greatness. His first step toward realizing his dream was enlisting in the Union Army. LEFT: Eliza Wetherby Otis ran the *Santa Barbara Weekly Press* while her husband was in Alaska. She also worked with him at the *Los Angeles Times*, writing poetry, domestic advice, and other articles.

CIVIL WAR AND NEW OPPORTUNITY

Otis found a job in Kentucky on the *Louisville Journal*. Kentucky was a border state, and the *Journal* opposed federal government interference with a state's right to permit slavery. But there were Republicans in the divided state, and Otis, who strongly opposed slavery, joined them as a delegate to the 1860 convention that nominated Abraham Lincoln for president. With Lincoln inaugurated, war broke out, and Otis enlisted as a private in an Ohio regiment in June of 1861. He fought in fifteen battles and was wounded at Winchester and Antietam. After the latter battle, he wrote his wife:

> All day the battle raged and today we rest upon the bank of the Antietam, near the Shepardstown Ferry on the Potomac. It would relieve me greatly could the sorely anxious heart of my faithful Lizzie be consoled by news of my safety.

Sometimes she followed Otis into the field and helped, in any way she could, to make his life more comfortable. When they were apart, she worried.

Otis was among the first to volunteer in the Civil War, which became the event by which he would measure the rest of this life. He saw action in fifteen major battles, among them Bull Run and Antietam, the war's bloodiest single-day conflict.

Otis rose to captain and, when he was discharged, was promoted to brevet lieutenant colonel by his commander, Rutherford B. Hayes, who later became president of the United States. One of the men serving over Otis was another future president, William McKinley. Wartime associations with both Hayes and McKinley would be helpful to Otis after his return to civilian life.

For Otis, the war was a life-changing event, as it was for the other veterans of the bloody combat—and for the nation itself. After the war, he and his wife ran a small-town newspaper in Ohio, but he also kept up his service ties at veteran's conventions and made enough political connections to land a job as the official reporter for the Ohio House of Representatives. His wartime friendship with Rutherford Hayes helped him win appointments to the Government Printing Office and the U.S. Patent Office in Washington, bureaucratic jobs that the young, ambitious combat veteran found unrewarding. He edited the *Grand Army Journal*, put out by the Grand Army of the Republic, an organization of veterans. He also wrote for the *Ohio Statesman*.

SEARCH FOR A TRUE VOCATION

None of these activities satisfied him. He was still searching for a career that would define his life. In 1874, his interest was piqued by an advertisement promoting a new business opportunity: raising angora goats in California. He and Lizzie took a trip west to explore the possibility. He decided against goats, but the Otises were left with a powerful impression of what they'd seen.

Otis hooked up with a fellow Ohian, W.W. Hollister, who moved west fleeing from debt and went on to become a millionaire rancher. Hollister wanted to start a paper, and in 1876 he told Otis that he wanted him to edit and run the new *Santa Barbara Weekly Press*. The Otises, by now the parents of three daughters, accepted. Hollister was a power in Santa Barbara, economically, politically and socially.

Despite Otis's best efforts, the *Santa Barbara Weekly Press* failed to prosper. He asked his old army chief, Rutherford Hayes, now U.S. president, for a top federal job in California, but U.S. Senator Aaron Sargent, unhappy over Otis's editorials attacking the Southern Pacific Railroad, blocked his appointment. The Southern Pacific controlled California—huge tracts of land, the governor, the legislature, city and county governments, as well as many newspapers. The S.P. was dubbed "the octopus," a perfect description for a company whose tentacles reached from its San Francisco headquarters to every

In March of 1876, Col. Otis took charge as editor of the *Santa Barbara Weekly Press*. The town was small and undeveloped, with two newspapers fighting for readers among two thousand residents. For four years, Otis and his wife Eliza struggled to keep it afloat but were unable to make a living.

part of the state. It took a lot of nerve to oppose the S.P., and Otis paid for his stand with the loss of a good job.

Otis finally did receive an appointment from Hayes, as a special agent in the Seal Islands of Alaska. While Otis was trying to stop poachers from killing seals and Eskimos from drinking alcohol, Eliza continued to run the *Press*, which was still doing poorly. She put aside the salary her husband sent her from Alaska, and, by the time he returned, she had saved enough to stake them to a new start in Los Angeles. "Otis soon realized that Santa Barbara was too small a place in which to materialize his dreams," wrote Thomas Storke, a later owner of the *Press* and one of California's most respected publishers.

A CITY RIPE FOR A REAL NEWSPAPER

In Los Angeles, the *Los Angeles Daily Times*, as it was then called, needed an editor. In 1882, Otis took the job at fifteen dollars a week. The paper was struggling financially, creating an opportunity for him to buy a stake in it. With the money he and Lizzie saved, plus wages owed him by the Santa Barbara paper, he bought fifteen percent of the *Times*.

Fortune was smiling when Otis arrived in town. Los Angeles was just emerging from a period of Old West lawlessness, which reached a peak in 1871 with the slaughter of nineteen Chinese people in a one-block unpaved alley, one of the worst examples of the racial hatred endemic to California. A Caucasian man, going to the aid of a policeman trying to break up a fight between Chinese gangs, was shot to death. What followed was a five-hour attack on the Chinese, ending with the massacre.

At the time of the incident, Chinese lived and worked in one-story adobe buildings amid a dangerous mixture of side businesses, including gambling, prostitution, and drug dealing. The street was known as *Calle de Los Negros*, so called because its residents were dark-skinned Californians of mixed race. These people, along with Mexicans and the few black residents, were scorned by the elite of Spanish and Mexican landowners and then by the Anglos, who called the street "Nigger Alley."

By the time Otis and his wife took over the *Times*, the incident had been tucked away in the history of an expanding city. It was an early example of how the city chose to bury its dark side in the sanctimonious belief that it, more than other places, represented the full potential of the American dream. The city that welcomed the Otises was described in a letter from a *Times* reader:

> There were no paved streets in the city, which during the rainy season, were in horrible condition, horses and vehicles often sinking knee-deep into the foul-smelling mixture of black mud and offal, which was churned by the vehicles

"I enter upon my journalistic duties in Los Angeles with a profound faith in the future development and sure destiny of the city. No city can offer superior inducements to Los Angeles as a field for business enterprise." —Harrison Gray Otis in 1882, the year he joined the *Times*.

General Otis riding in a rickshaw in Los Angeles's original Chinatown. The neighborhood was later razed to make way for Union Station, and a new Chinatown sprang up northeast of the original one.

and hoofs into the consistency of a sticky paste . . .. The "sidewalks" were little better in most places, consisting mostly of gravel, which after a long rain got so mixed with the soil that you could not tell one from the other.

The most important of the few buildings was located several blocks south of where the Chinese massacre occurred. It was the two-story Clocktower Courthouse, where lawyers conducted business for new and more peaceful clients, immigrants from the East and Midwest in search of farms or city lots for homes and businesses. "The only staple of commerce or merchandise was real estate," said Henry O'Melveny, who started his law office in Los Angeles in 1881.

The Southern Pacific had extended its tracks into Los Angeles in 1876. The Santa Fe would arrive ten years later. The railroads gave the city its first direct connection with the Southwest, Midwest, and East. The S.P. powered its way into Los Angeles with the cooperation of lawyer O'Melveny's father and other town notables promoting the land boom. The railroad demanded a subsidy from the city, and the proposal was put to a citywide vote. O'Melveny recalled in a memoir how the anti-railroad forces paid Mexican Americans, then a majority of the city's population, to vote against the city's financial support of the railroad. According to *Lawyers of Los Angeles*, "The pro-railroad people during the night . . . offered a larger price and bought the votes for the pro-railroad proposition." It won by a vote of 1,896 to 650. The violent outlaws of past years had been replaced by a different kind of opportunism.

Harrison Gray Otis was one of these opportunists, and soon became their leader. Toughened by the war, hungering for the success he had not yet achieved, he saw Los Angeles as the opportunity that had long eluded him. As he said at the time,

It is the fattest land I ever was in by many degrees. Climate and real estate make a most intoxicating mixture here in Los Angeles. Just enough has been done with the varied and rich resources to show the mighty possibilities of the region. There is nothing like it.

A CHANDLER COMES TO THE TIMES

In 1885, Harry Chandler went to work for Otis in the *Times'* circulation department. In 1883, Harry had left New Hampshire, where, as a Dartmouth undergraduate, he had contracted a severe lung ailment. As was the customary treatment for "lungers," as they were called, he was sent to California for a dry-weather cure. But even in this more favorable climate, his hacking cough got him thrown out of several boardinghouses. Los Angeles, he later recalled, struck him as "a crude little frontier town." Discour-

In the late nineteenth century, the country was hearing more and more about California's lush, moderate climate, famous for its agricultural marvels as well as its curative powers. Stories circulated about the area's rich farmland—supposedly capable of yielding enormous crops with little effort from farmers. Fine farmland was abundant, but for farm laborers raising good crops still meant spending long days in the hot sun.

aged, he walked the city's streets, lonely and homesick.

It wasn't long before his luck changed. As one of his daughters later wrote, "wandering through the streets he chanced to see in the window of a photographer a collection of portraits of beautiful children. Among these he was astonished to see one of himself whispering into the ear of a little girl. He bought the picture—a stereoscopic slide—and kept it as a souvenir. He claimed it cured his loneliness." He met a doctor also afflicted with a lung ailment, who gave him a job in his fruit orchard. The enterprising young man sold extra fruit to farm laborers and, after accumulating three thousand dollars, went home to the East.

His sickness recurred back East, so he returned to Los Angeles. In 1885 he took a job as a clerk in the circulation department of the *Times*. By year's end he had worked his way up to head of the department. Things were also going well for Harry on a personal level. He met the lovely Magdalena Schlador, whose brother worked at the paper, and the couple married three years later.

As circulation boss, Chandler's job was to increase the number of subscribers from an anemic 1,100. He recruited carrier boys he could depend on. In 1941, Chandler described those early days in a *Times* article:

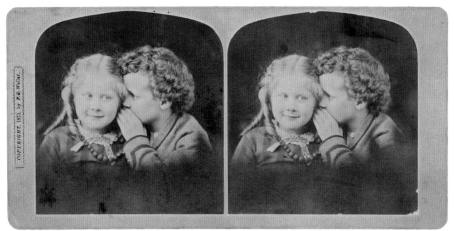

As a child growing up poor in a small New Hampshire town, Harry Chandler sometimes earned a little money working as a model for a local photographer. Down on his luck in Los Angeles, Harry was surprised to see this picture of himself in a stereopticon shop.

> When I took over the circulation job for the *Times* I bought the routes and then had boys deliver the papers. They used to ride saddle horses at first and then later on, when bicycles were introduced, they used them . . . They got up at 3:30 in the morning so they could get busy at 4. They learned to be punctual, honest and thrifty. Yet the parents of some wouldn't let their sons be newspaper carriers. They thought it was beneath their dignity. Nowadays, though, the boys who were the carriers are the real leaders of Los Angeles in business and finance and law.

Placing such a high priority on discipline, reliability, and hard work, the young circulation manager was obviously a stern taskmaster as he built up the circulation. He collected money from subscribers and made sure they received their papers. "I used to collect for the paper in all kinds of strange places," Chandler recalled. "I remember that E.L. Doheny, later the millionaire oil man, was hand drilling an oil well out at the old Second Street Park when I went to get his money for the *Times*."

As diligent as he was in chasing down customers, Harry Chandler had something else that served him well—an entrepreneurial temperament along with ambition that matched that of Otis. A business partner had bought a competing newspaper, the *Los Angeles Herald*. "He and Colonel Otis always were having a terrible scrap in the papers, as was quite normal in those days,

Harry Chandler started with the *Los Angeles Times* in 1885 as a clerk in the circulation department. Pneumonia and then bronchitis had forced him to drop out of Dartmouth and come west seeking a cure. His illness resulted from a dive he made on a dare into a vat of ice-covered starch.

and it got so at last that my ex-partner became quite violent toward the colonel." Chandler wrote in his *Times* account of that period in the paper's history.

> This made me pretty mad. We used to pull all kinds of tricks on one another in the newspaper business and think nothing of it— it was just a custom—and I decided now was the time for one of them. Through a friend I secretly bought the circulation routes of the *Herald*, entirely unknown, of course, to my ex-partner. Then I hired a big tallyho and one day shipped off the entire *Herald* circulation and carrier crew to the San Bernardino Mountains for a five-day holiday. When the time came to distribute the *Herald* . . . there weren't any boys to do it and the confusion was so great for the next few days that the *Times* put on a subscription campaign and got about half of the subscribers. That kind of thing made life exciting, and as it might be the other fellow's turn the next day, hard feelings did not last long.

Chandler also acquired the circulation route of another Otis enemy, Colonel Henry Boyce, publisher of the *Tribune*. Boyce and Otis had been partners in purchasing the *Times* but couldn't get along, and Otis bought him out. Chandler, with his control of circulation routes, put the *Tribune* out of business and then secretly bought the dead newspaper's plant, subscription lists, and circulation routes. Otis, worried about a new competitor, asked Chandler to dig out the name of the buyer and make a deal with him. Chandler told Otis that he was the buyer.

"Such men as Harry Chandler do not grow on every bush," Colonel Otis said. "He is a sly fox—a brainy and resourceful man capable of large achievements. He is the best friend I have on earth."

In 1892, seven years after he joined the *Times*, Chandler's wife, Magdalena, died after childbirth. The young widower then courted and married Otis's daughter, Marian, the only one of the three Otis children, all girls, who worked at the paper. Best friend to his father-in-law and his right-hand man, Chandler became *Times* business manager. They were a perfect combination to run Los Angeles: the blustery public personality and the shrewd behind-the-scenes dealmaker.

In 1889 Harry married the beautiful Magdalena Schlador of Galveston, Texas. She died of puerperal fever at the age of twenty-nine in 1892, two weeks after the birth of their second daughter. BELOW: Harry married Marian Otis, the publisher's daughter, on June 5, 1894. Marian, who worked as the business office secretary at the paper, gave up her job to care for his two young daughters.

The New General

A few years later, in 1898, the Spanish-American War broke out, and Otis wanted to return to the battlefield. He asked his old army colleague, President William McKinley, for an assignment. By then, Otis had become one of the most powerful men in Southern California and a controversial character in both the northern and southern parts of the state. When McKinley made Otis a brigadier general, opponents tried to block his appointment, but the president got his way. Leaving the paper in the hands

of his wife and son-in-law, Otis went off to war. He led troops fighting in the Philippines and remained after the war ended to put down a revolt by Filipino nationalists. The battles were fierce. "The dead fell like soldiers at their posts of duty defending the laws of the Republic, and the wounded suffer that the flag may continue to fly triumphant over territory won by the national arms from a foreign foe," General Otis later wrote.

When he returned from the war, he was greeted by four thousand in Los Angeles. For the rest of his life, he emulated a military style. He called his homes the Bivouac and the Outpost and had the *Times* building designed to looked like a fortress. Otis kept rifles and loaded shotguns in the building, but not enough, as it turned out later, to save the building from bombing by his enemies.

Combat experience, his years as a frontier printer and journalist, his time in Washington, and his Republican Party activism had given him the experience and competitive edge he needed to dominate the city. The self-doubt he had expressed in his letters to Eliza as a bridegroom was not evident as he put out the newspaper each day. His uninhibited writing style, full of insults and an excess of adjectives, screamed for attention.

"Fair" does not describe his presentation of the news—few of the frontier editors were fair. But he did understand how to use editorial content to build circulation. Eliza's poems, columns, and news of religion, women's life, literature, and culture broadened the paper's appeal. There was also, historian Ann Gorman Condon observed, a "great ideology af-

Otis was in his early sixties when he volunteered to fight in the Spanish-American War. Promoted to brigadier general, he was sent to the Philippines. The unit he commanded was instrumental in winning the battle of Caloocan, which led to the fall of Manila.

finity between Otis's newspaper and the hosts of migrants who flowed into Southern California." They shared the intense post-Civil War patriotism invoked by Eliza's poetry and Otis's editorials. "Equally strong in the mind of the Otises and their readers was their belief in the unfolding progress of America and its special destiny, guided by the firm standards of Protestant morality," Condon wrote.

Above all, Otis had a sense of what would sell. When a young man in Ohio, Charles Fletcher Lummis, wrote in 1884 that he was going to walk from his home state to California and offered to send the *Times* articles as he made his way west, Otis took him up on it. He understood how the articles would appeal to a town filled with people who had made the same journey, albeit by train. In fact, Otis greeted Lummis, by then a local celebrity because of his stories, when he arrived and hired him to be city editor.

The railroad-fed boom of the 1880s was petering out toward the end of the decade. Otis had built the *Los Angeles Times*—no longer the *Los Angeles Daily Times*—into the city's most influential newspaper, and he was the foremost leader of the Republican Party with clout in Congress and the White House. Before his arrival, Los Angeles had been run by a small group of conservative lawyers and business people. After he came into power, the group remained small but he was the dominant figure. When Otis talked—or, more likely, shouted—these men listened. When he proposed the creation of a Los Angeles Chamber of Commerce in 1888, they agreed, and although E.W. Jones was the chamber's president, Otis, as second vice-president, had the real power.

The chamber's goal, as a 1915 article in *Colliers Magazine* pointed out, was to bring a certain kind of person to Los Angeles, people in the Otis and Chandler mold. The chamber, said writer Peter Clark McFarland, "built the city. It even picked out the kind of people it wanted to live in the city—the well-to-do farmers, merchants and mechanics of the Mississippi Valley—men close enough to the pioneer line to have courage, initiative and adaptability."

A recovering tubercular immigrant from the Midwest, Frank Wiggins, was the chamber's publicity man. His assignment was to bring in trainloads of Midwesterners. He sent exhibits around the country, California on Wheels, featuring Southern California's fruits and vegetables. He even had a larger-than-life elephant built for the 1893 Chicago World's Fair, made of wire over a wooden frame and

Like the Annual Midwinter Number, this Midsummer Number of the *Los Angeles Times* was designed to attract Easterners and Midwesterners to Southern California.

"YOU'RE EITHER WITH ME OR AGAINST ME."
—HARRISON GRAY OTIS

covered with 15,000 large California walnuts. The rail-roads joined in with advertisements and a fare war. On one day, Santa Fe offered a one-dollar ticket to Los Angeles from Kansas City.

A Free Harbor to Build a Powerful City

What Los Angeles needed was an expanded harbor for the trade that would be coming. In the opinion of Otis, Chandler, and their associates, the city also needed to be freed from the grip of "the octopus," the Southern Pacific Railroad.

The S.P. and its president, Collis P. Huntington, wanted monopoly control of the harbor. Otis, Chandler, and the other Los Angeles powers wanted a free harbor that would be open to all. They also believed the old harbor was inadequate for the huge city they had in mind. It occupied shallow mud flats with a long pier to allow trains to reach deeper waters where freighters docked, mostly with cargos of lumber and a limited number of passengers.

Otis, his newspaper, and the Chamber of Commerce took on the Southern Pacific. "Los Angeles is at present free of Southern Pacific domination, but that corporation is slowly tightening its coils about us," said Otis. "Let us not be jostled off our feet by the chicanery and bribe-giving attempts of a mendacious monopoly." Otis unrelent-

Harry Chandler in his first car, parked in front of the *Times* circulation department. He was an early advocate of the automobile and the possibilities it offered. Later, he would work to bring auto and tire plants to Southern California. OPPOSITE: Otis was fascinated by all things military, and these swords were part of his collection of two thousand weapons. Included were a gun from Custer's last stand, a crossbow from the Boxer Rebellion, and a pike dating back to the Crusades.

ingly mocked Huntington in the pages of the paper, calling him "Uncle Collis" and, in one especially demeaning headline, awarding him a marble heart. Otis, having fought the S.P. while in Santa Barbara, knew the enemy well and understood how to defeat "the octopus." According to historian William Deverell, Otis and his colleagues were "using political enmity toward the Southern Pacific to their economic and political advantage. And they're taking an old story, a David-and-Goliath story, and making it the story of Los Angeles's possibilities for the twentieth century. And they win."

Despite their belief in private enterprise, Otis and the others asked the federal government to build a sea wall that would turn the mud flats into a deep-water harbor. It was a huge amount of money for the time, between four and five million dollars. Although the Los Angeles chieftains were Republicans, they won the invaluable support of the state's Democratic senator, Stephen Mallory White, who emerged from a quiet Senate career to shock his colleagues and California by opposing Huntington and his railroad. In June 1896, legislation clearing the way for construction of the Los Angeles harbor became law. After a long fight in the Senate, Congress appropriated money for the harbor in San Pedro. Otis had beaten the Southern Pacific, and Los Angeles had its free harbor.

WATER: KEY TO GROWTH AND WEALTH

All Los Angeles needed now was water to support a larger population. There was a source, more than two hundred miles to the north in the Owens Valley on the other side of the Sierra Nevada.

The meandering Los Angeles River, in addition to artesian wells that drew water from vast underground sources, supplied water to Los Angeles and the ranches and farms in the flatlands around it. Heavy pumping from wells drastically lowered

A *Times* story proclaims victory in the battle for a free harbor. General Otis was not above using his paper for character assassination. OPPOSITE TOP: After a bitter disagreement, General Otis prevailed over Huntington in the dispute over Los Angeles Harbor. Here Otis poses at a war memorial with a view of the new harbor behind him. OPPOSITE BOTTOM: Spectators watch the completion of a breakwater, needed for the harbor.

VICTORY !

San Pedro Gets the Deep-water Harbor

And Uncle Collis is Given the Marble Heart.

The Government Won't Build Him a Breakwater.

THE OLD MAN IS CRUSHED.

Aging Sadly Under His Many Reverses.

He Tried to Run a Bluff on Secretary Lamont.

But Daniel Would not Listen to the Old Sinner.

THE HARBOR BOARD'S REPORT.

Commissioner Morgan Did not Sign it, but All the Others Did—Every Point at Issue Decided in Favor of San Pedro.

[BY THE TIMES' SPECIAL WIRE.]

the underground water tables. The river could be an unreliable source, flooding in the wet season, sometimes reduced to creek size during dry periods. Open ditches, called *zanjas*, brought water from the river to Los Angeles homes and businesses—delivering unwanted fish, too, that sometimes found their way into the *Times'* water-powered press. From the mountains to the Pacific Ocean, Southern California was too dry to support a large population—fine for the cattle ranching and agriculture that had drawn the Spanish colonists, but not suitable for a city of the scale that Otis and Chandler had in mind.

The population was growing, reaching 102,479 in 1900. Otis, Chandler and his cohorts in the Chamber of Commerce had ambitions beyond the existing city limits of Los Angeles if they could import more water. The water would permit business and residential development on land they would buy. Los Angeles would grow and flourish.

Yet the group's methods—virtually cheating Owens Valley ranchers out of their water rights—was an act of political and economic brutality that has lingered in the city's history. This chapter of L.A. history is recalled in Robert Towne's script for the 1974 film *Chinatown*. Although it is not entirely historically accurate, the film's title has become a synonym for municipal corruption and private greed.

The story of how L.A. found the water to make the city's enormous growth possible may have begun with Fred Eaton, an associate of Otis and Chandler. It was Eaton who had the vision and shrewdness to formulate a plan and put it into action. Trained as an engineer, Eaton was superintendent of the Los Angeles City Water Company. He favored public ownership of this utility, and, in 1902, after he became mayor of Los Angeles, he succeeded in persuading the city to buy the water company.

Eaton's friend William Mulholland came over from the water company to run the new municipal operation, and Eaton arranged a trip to the Owens Valley to show Mulholland how the river could supply the city with water. They traveled by buckboard. "A classical poet writing the history of Los Angeles in the style of Virgil's *Aeneid* might very well see in this buckboard journey across the desert a symbolic journey into Los Angeles's future," historian Kevin Starr observed. "A comic poet would note the trail of empty liquor bottles left behind and see in this ribbon of glass the first mapping of the aqueduct route."

Eaton passed word of the advantages of Owens Valley water to other influential men in Los Angeles. These insiders understood that, if things were done quietly, Eaton could buy the water rights from unsuspecting farmers and other landowners in the Owens Valley. Of course, not a word of it appeared in the pages of the *Los Angeles Times*. The reason is obvious: General Otis and Harry Chandler were part of the intrigue. Aware of Eaton's activities and approving them, Otis, Chandler, and a group of city leaders formed a land investment partnership in 1903 and purchased an option to buy sixteen thousand acres of San Fernando Valley that would be irrigated by Owens River water. Otis's rival publisher, E.T. Earl, was part of the partnership, as was streetcar magnate Moses Sherman, who was a member of the city water board.

OPPOSITE: Once the new harbor was under construction, the route to it was annexed to Los Angeles. With the harbor and a railroad station operating, Angelenos flocked to the new facility in 1908.

Enlisting Federal Help

Eaton bought up Owens Valley water rights, pretending it was for a federal reclamation project that would help the area's residents. At the same time, he used his pull to persuade the federal government to put its own water reclamation plan for the Owens Valley aside and allow the water to be sent over the Sierras to Los Angeles. When the federal government agreed, the *Times* immediately broke the story. "Titanic Project to Give City A River," was the headline.

ABOVE: A panorama of the rural Owens Valley reveals the Sierras, source of the water that would someday benefit Los Angeles. LEFT: Moses Sherman and Harry Chandler, partners in two land syndicates in the San Fernando Valley. Because railroad magnate Sherman was on the Los Angeles water board when decisions were made about building the aqueduct, some accused him of conflict of interest. RIGHT: Harry Chandler and William Mulholland hold a survey map of the roads required for contractors to carry building materials for the aqueduct. A total of 505 miles of roads and trails were constructed for the purpose.

The article failed to mention that Otis, Chandler, and their partners in the land investment group stood to profit from the deal. A few days later, the rival *Los Angeles Examiner* ran an exposé of the land speculation partnership and listed its members. But that didn't stop the project from moving ahead.

Scholar Abe Hoffman, a respected San Fernando Valley historian, said: "They basically had insider information from Moses Sherman. He's a member of the Board of Water Commissioners and he's also on this formation of the land syndicate that's going to buy land in the San Fernando Valley. Next thing you know, the land syndicate is utilizing that information for the first of the great real-estate ventures in the San Fernando Valley. And they have it in the general area where the aqueduct would end."

Owens Valley residents belatedly learned they had been tricked into selling their water rights. They protested to Washington, declaring that water from the Owens River should not irrigate the San Fernando Valley. But they ran

into a powerful foe—President Teddy Roosevelt, America's foremost advocate of public water projects. To him, the aqueduct seemed to exemplify the Progressive goal of efficient delivery of needed services to the people, favoring the many rather than the few.

Los Angeles, in his opinion, needed the water more than the Owens Valley. Roosevelt personally removed restrictions on Los Angeles's use of the water from legislation authorizing the city's aqueduct to cross federal land. The congressman representing the Owens Valley told Roosevelt he wanted to discuss the matter, and the president replied, "You don't need to talk. I am doing the talking." When Mulholland returned to Los Angeles after the Washington triumph, he told a crowd waiting for him at the railroad depot, "We got what we wanted."

Once the aqueduct was built, Los Angeles was on its way to becoming the great city of General Otis's dreams. On a single day, May 22, 1915, the city tripled in size by annexing the San Fernando Valley—an area of a hundred thousand acres—as contemplated by the aqueduct backers, as well as gaining an area west of downtown called Palms. This gave the city the financial heft to sell the bonds needed to complete the water project.

When voters approved the bond issue, a headline in the *Los Angeles Times* called it the "Greatest Achievement in History of the City." Half a page was devoted to a map of the newly annexed land with another headline reading, "Splendid Realization Crowns Los Angeles's Vision of Municipal Destiny."

Hearing of well-paid jobs building the aqueduct, workers arrived from as far away as Bulgaria, Serbia, Switzerland, and Greece. OPPOSITE: As water arrived from the Owens Valley, engineer William Mulholland addressed the assembled crowd with one of the most memorable quotes in Los Angeles history: "There it is. Take it!"

A motorist stops to take in the view of Los Angeles from Lookout Mountain. Even in 1912, the air was hazy.

SYMBOL OF GOOD AND EVIL

The $23 million aqueduct—expensive for the era—was one of the West's engineering marvels. Mulholland figured that gravity would carry the water to the San Fernando Valley, and it did. The aqueduct was completed in 1913, five years after construction started, just as Mulholland had promised. Five thousand men worked on the project and "crews of mining roustabouts battled smallpox, typhoid and 130-degree days," wrote Kevin Roderick. It took 1,239 days to dig a five-mile tunnel through solid rock.

But many lives were lost in completing the big western water projects and the Los Angeles Aqueduct offered a tragic example of that. Even after the aqueduct was completed, Mulholland built dams and reservoirs to store the water. Fearing sabotage and earthquakes, in 1925 Mulholland started work on a dam big enough to hold a year's supply of water. The St. Francis Dam, completed in 1926, was located in San Francisquito Canyon, above the San Fernando Valley. The walls of the canyon were porous and water seeped through. Responding to leaks which had appeared on March 12, 1928, Mulholland and his chief assistant, Harvey Van Norman, inspected the dam. They pronounced it safe and returned to Los Angeles. A few hours later, when almost all of the residents of the area were asleep, the dam burst. The water was a hundred feet high when it roared down San Francisquito Canyon and into the channel of the Santa Clara River, heading toward the Pacific Ocean. It swept through the little communities of Piru, Fillmore, and Santa Paula, past Saticoy and Montalvo, and finally to the sea. The flood killed at least 450 people, wrecked 12,240 homes, and ruined 7,900 acres of farmland. Mulholland, a broken man, was forced into retirement. "I envy the dead," he said.

The Owens Valley aqueduct has remained a powerful symbol of the good and evil involved in the building of Los Angeles. From the beginning, it smacked of a shady deal. With the newspaper's complicit silence, Eaton lied his way through the Owens Valley, buying up water rights for Los Angeles, leaving part of the area dry and dusty. In the history of the West, such underhanded dealing might be excused as another example of the dirty tricks that were part of the region's bitter water wars. There was no excuse for the proprietors of the *Los Angeles Times*, the area's leading newspaper, not covering it. They and their fellow investors profited by selling and developing land in the San Fernando Valley. The episode stained the *Times*.

Still, the public works and their own private enterprises promoted in the pages of their newspaper remain an important part of life in the twenty-first century. The harbor that General Otis created is one of the Southland's great generators of jobs and commerce, with trucks, planes, and trains carrying goods into the Central Valley and past the California border into neighboring states and beyond. Water continues to flow through the aqueduct, which was supplemented by another one in 1970, feeding residential subdivisions, malls, movie studios, factories, apartment houses, universities, and high-rise office buildings in a city that no doubt has exceeded even the imaginations of General Otis and Harry Chandler. The road there wasn't pretty. The *Times* has had a lot to live down. So has the city of Los Angeles, which in recent years has been forced by the courts to repair at least some of the environmental damage inflicted on the Owens Valley. Even so, it all worked. The L.A. that Otis and Chandler invented has endured and, for the most part, flourished.

Despite his accomplishments, General Otis had many detractors. Historian Morrow Mayo wrote of him: "The military bee buzzed incessantly in his bonnet. He was a holy terror in his newspaper plant; his natural voice was that of a game-warden roaring at seal poachers."
LEFT: This New Year's Day 1898 edition was designed to attract new industry to Los Angeles.

Between 1880 and 1910, the population of Los Angeles grew from 12,000 to 320,000.

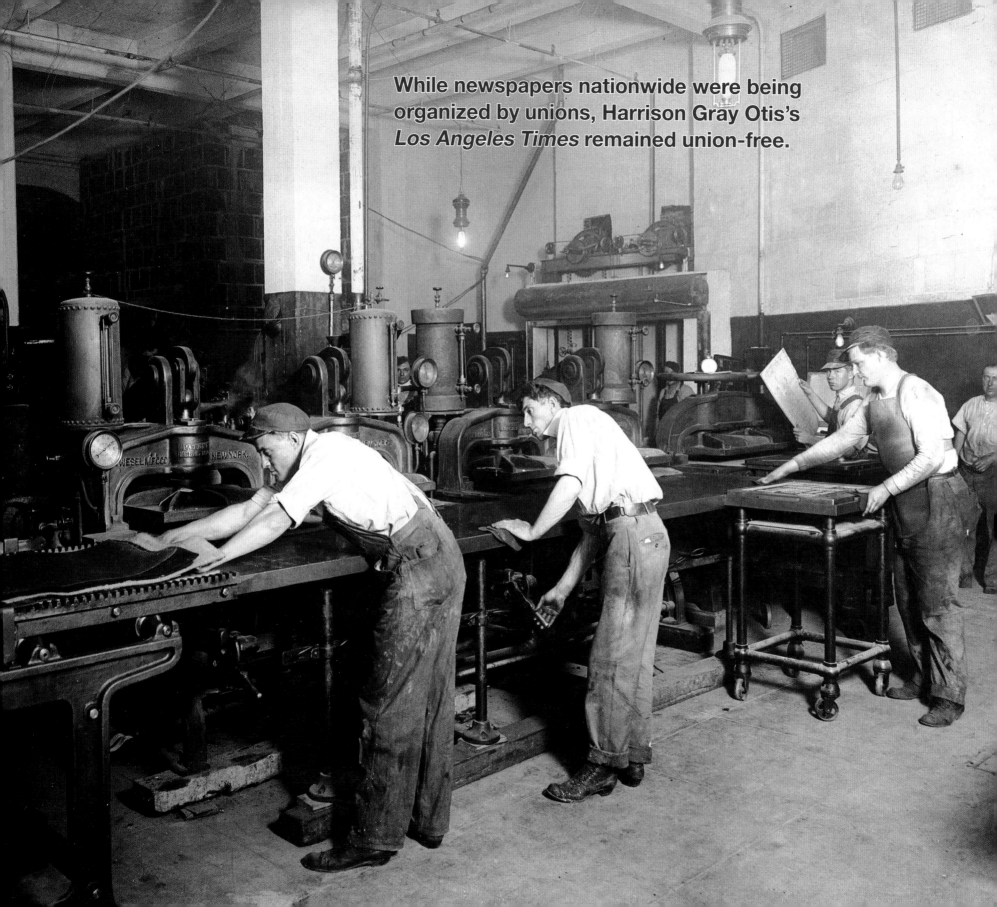

While newspapers nationwide were being organized by unions, Harrison Gray Otis's *Los Angeles Times* remained union-free.

"In the conduct of the *Times*, always place public and private morality and the true interests of the city before mere commercialism or material success." —Harrison Gray Otis

"YOU ANARCHIC SCUM. YOU COWARDLY MURDERERS, YOU MIDNIGHT ASSASSINS, YOU WHOSE HANDS ARE DRIPPING WITH THE INNOCENT BLOOD OF YOUR VICTIMS, HAVE COMMITTED ONE OF THE WORST ATROCITIES IN THE HISTORY OF THE WORLD."

—GEN. HARRISON GRAY OTIS

CHAPTER TWO

The Bombing

General Harrison Gray Otis's thundering reaction to the bombing of the *Los Angeles Times* on October 1, 1910 was to reflect the paper's attitude toward unions, liberal thought, and dissent for many decades—through two world wars, a depression, and into an era when such views were out of touch with modern Los Angeles.

Words, the old master of vitriol knew, have power. "Which is the better," he had asked Pomona College students five years before, "a narrative written, a statement drawn in strong, clear, clean-cut familiar Anglo-Saxon, making every word weigh a pound or a narrative written in a 'sissy' style, feebly and inadequately bringing out the points of the story or statement?"

Pound upon pound of words came out of the *Times* plant before and long after the bombing, excoriating unions and their

General Otis, who was out of town at the time of the bombing, inspects the ruins and points out the destruction to some in the gathered crowd. PAGES 42-43: In 1908, downtown Los Angeles was bustling with business and plenty of street life. PAGE 44: Pressmen work at creating stereo plates, molded forms of the day's news pages, to put on the presses. PAGE 45: Printers create news pages using lines of metal type in the composing room. General Otis was proud of his modern equipment and named his printing presses Uncle Sam, Columbia, and The Old Guard. PAGE 46: General Otis with opera star Ellen Beach Yaw, who sang the national anthem at the opening of the Los Angeles Aqueduct. There were rumors that she and the general were having an affair. PAGE 47: A family picnic at General Otis's spread, the Tejon Ranch. The general is standing in the center; the laughing woman at the right is Harry's daughter Francesca.

allies, defining political debate in the starkest terms, leaving no room for compromise. Los Angeles became known among union members and liberal political activists as "Otistown," home of the open shop. *Open shop* was the term used to describe a factory or workplace where union membership was not a requirement to work. It also meant there were no union contracts to interfere with the autonomy of employers.

The paper was the premier voice of the Republican Party in California. It was also the strongest voice against organized labor and all liberal or leftist ideas. But, as Otis understood, words couldn't do the job of defeating these elements without some help. In addition to its bombastic editorials and slanted news stories, the *Times* tried, often successfully, to control politics and government so it could accomplish its goals through legislation. It picked Republican candidates and kept Democrats out of its news columns. Its political writers—disdainfully called "trained seals" by other journalists—actually used hand signals to tell Los Angeles City Council members and state legislators how to vote on specific bills. Otis organized a booster group, the Merchants and Manufacturers Association, whose main purpose was union busting. Its members made sure credit was denied to businesses that negotiated with unions. Otis and his followers mobilized every influential institution in the city behind the cause. The most powerful of these was the corrupt Los Angeles Police Department, which promoted a culture of brutality, secretiveness, and racism that took years to eliminate.

Bombing the *Times*

The bombing of the *Times* occurred at 1 A.M. on Saturday, October 1, 1910. "With the suddenness of an earthquake, an explosion, which the dry snappy sound left no room to doubt of its origin in dynamite, tore down the whole first floor of the building on Broadway, just back of the entrance to the business office," the paper reported in a one-page edition put together early that morning.

Rescuers were driven back by the flames. ". . . [A]lthough they could hear clearly the cries of distress, the groans and screams of the men and women who, mangled and crippled by flying debris from the explosion lay imprisoned by the flames, about to be cremated alive. Along the windows of the editorial and city rooms, on the south side of the building, through a choking volume of black smoke could be seen men and women crowding each

Front page of *The Los Angeles Times'* bombing issue. Otis had established a nearby auxiliary printing plant after the 1906 earthquake and fire in San Francisco, but the remaining news staff had only a few hours before the morning paper's deadline. At the invitation of the *Los Angeles Herald*, *Times* editors and reporters walked to the *Herald*'s offices and began writing up their accounts of the bombing. OPPOSITE: The blast of the *Times* explosion could be heard throughout Los Angeles. Crowds thronged to the scene by carriage, streetcar, or on foot—whatever means they had—to gape at the flames consuming the fortress-like structure.

other about the windows of the third floor. The cries for ladders went up, frantic." At the time of the explosion, General Otis was returning from a trip to Mexico.

     Harry Chandler had left the building before the bomb went off. "He rushed in to rescue his imprisoned employees but was driven back . . . " his paper reported. "He gathered his faithful around him and with tears streaming down his face thanked God for those who were saved. 'The hounds,' he cried. 'My poor men.' Then he hurried to the receiving hospital." Twenty-one had been killed. "They can kill our men and can wreck our buildings but by the God above, they cannot kill the *Times*," Harry E. Andrews, the managing editor, wrote in an editorial that morning.

     A bomb was also placed near Otis's house. With the general in Mexico, his grandson was spending the night at the Otis house. "My father was sleeping in his grandfather's bedroom and bed," said Otis Booth, the general's great-grandson. "He heard a ticking sound outside of the window; windows were open in that era before air conditioning. The household looked at what was there, called the police and the police took a package they had found into an open part of the park where it exploded . . . I would not be here to tell this story if my father hadn't heard the strange noise and acted."

     The bombing occurred after a long labor dispute. In 1890, the real estate and construction boom of the late 1880s collapsed. With the dip in the economy, the *Times* and the city's other three papers had cut wages by twenty percent, provoking a strike. The other papers settled, but Otis refused to yield, putting out the paper for years with non-union printers. His goal was to eliminate unions altogether from the city of Los Angeles.

Workmen begin cleaning up the debris left by the tremendous blast. The casket on the ground contains the charred body of one of the bomb's twenty-one fatalities. OPPOSITE: The shell of the *Times* building is still smoldering the day after the disaster.

Funeral of Harvey Elder, assistant city editor of the *Times*. To escape the flames, he hung from his hands from a window ledge, the paper reported, "until the leaping flame behind him curled out across his face . . . then he dropped, horribly burned, senseless and crushed into the life net below."

This would satisfy his ideology and give Los Angeles an economic advantage over San Francisco, where unions had raised wages.

Battle Against Unions

By 1910, Otis and the Merchants and Manufacturers Association had expanded their goal and were engaged in a full-scale battle against national unions. Organized labor retaliated by picketing the *Times* building and boycotting the paper. Backed by Otis and other businessmen, the Los Angeles City Council passed an anti-picketing ordinance. The police department vigorously enforced it, and 472 picketers were arrested. This was the beginning of an unholy alliance between the police department and the *Times*. If the cops would beat up and arrest strikers, the paper would overlook police involvement in graft—payoffs for prostitution and gambling—except when corruption was too ugly for the paper to ignore.

Leading the union effort was the well-organized International Association of Bridge and Structural Iron Workers, which, along with the other metal trades unions, was demanding an eight-hour day and a four-dollar daily minimum wage, up from the two dollars and fifty cents that the ironworkers were paid. The union had already planted bombs at several plants around the country, but these had exploded without fatalities. When Los Angeles strike leaders asked the national union's secretary-treasurer, John J. McNamara, for help, he sent his brother Jim, a dynamiter who had successfully bombed other union targets.

Historian Geoffrey Cowan wrote, "As night fell on the city, Jim McNamara planted a suitcase containing sixteen sticks of eighty percent dynamite in the alleyway behind the *Times*." He set the timer for 1 A.M. and then planted a second bomb at General Otis's home and another at the home of Felix Zeehandelaar, the secretary of the Merchants and Manufacturers Association, before catching a train to San Francisco." His intent appeared to be for the bomb at the *Times*' building to explode in a spot where no one would be working. "He didn't realize," Cowan went on, that "he had left the explosives in an alley behind the *Times* where ink was stored. The bomb ignited the ink, causing the huge damage and loss of life."

TRIAL OF THE McNamara Brothers

By chance, the famous detective William Burns arrived in Los Angeles to deliver a speech the morning of the bombing. As Cowan described it, the mayor, hearing Burns was in town, visited his hotel and asked the detective to solve the crime "no matter what the cost and no matter who they [the dynamiters] are." Burns replied, "I already have a good idea who is responsible for this outrage." He suspected J.J. McNamara and the iron workers union. He had been investigating them for a similar explosion. It took him months, but in April of 1911, Burns and his team of detectives arrested the McNamara brothers and Ortie McManigal, a union official also involved in dynamiting. McManigal confessed to taking part in the bombings and implicated the McNamaras. The

General Otis's *Times* was one of a number of businesses that provided jobs for skilled workers, like these pressmen. In his view, he had a special relationship with his workers. He believed that his employees, whom he called "the phalanx," were well paid and well provided for; he was loyal to them as they were to him. He also believed the phalanx disliked the unions as much as he did.

American Federation of Labor and its leader, Samuel Gompers, took charge of the defense and hired Clarence Darrow, who had successfully defended other union leaders, to represent the brothers. Also on the defense team was Job Harriman, a socialist who was running for mayor of Los Angeles.

As the trial approached, the brilliant Darrow turned publicity about the trial away from the fate of the dynamite victims to the circumstances surrounding the arrest of the elder McNamara, John, the union secretary. He had been arrested during a union meeting in Indianapolis, hustled out of the state, and taken to California. "He was clearly kidnapped," Darrow said, in a line meant to appeal to working people suspicious of police and bosses. He also pointed out that John was a non-drinking, religious Catholic.

This portrayal resonated with many Angelenos who either failed to read the *Times* or didn't believe its stories. A month after the bombing, some fifteen thousand participated in a parade supporting labor. In the Socialist paper, *Appeal To Reason*, party leader Eugene Debs said:

> The *Times* and its crowd of union-haters are themselves the instigators if not the actual perpetrators of that crime and the murderers of the twenty human beings who perished as its victims.

Not all of the city's establishment blindly followed the *Times*. Attorney Joseph Scott, president of both the Board of Education and the Chamber of Commerce, joined Darrow's defense team, an action that gave an immeasurable boost to the McNamara cause. Scott, a British immigrant with an Irish Catholic mother, sympathized with the McNamaras, whose lives reminded him of his own. "My friends pleaded with me to keep out of the case," he said. Knowing he would never be forgiven by Otis, one friend said, "Joe, you're the town's fair-haired boy . . . please don't do it." But Scott thought that, "Under a lawyer's oath the meanest man among us is entitled to a defense."

Seated in the courtroom during the trial are Clarence Darrow's co-counsel Joseph Scott, Jim McNamara, Darrow, and co-counsel LeCompte Davis. Although the trial would end badly for Darrow and the men he was defending, the lead lawyer looks confident, and his figure dominates the scene. Later, he was accused of attempting to bribe a juror. OPPOSITE: The McNamara brothers, in dark suits and hats, are brought to the courthouse by sheriff's deputies and men from the Burns detective agency. William F. Burns, America's most famous detective, engaged in a six-month manhunt before obtaining a confession from a union leader.

While Otis blustered away in editorials, Harry Chandler assessed the political situation and worried. Job Harriman of the McNamara defense team was now running strongly in the race for mayor. Chandler wrote to Otis, who was in Washington, that their foes "are doing the most that the active use of money and devilish scheming can do to change public sentiment their way here. They are sending a copy of *Appeal to Reason* to every resident of Southern California and claim they are going to continue until after the trial of the dynamiters is concluded." He warned that, "Our solicitors going through East Los Angeles and Boyle Heights find that from thirty to fifty percent of the apparently intelligent people whom they call upon are filled up with the socialistic and anarchistic idea that these men are innocent and that Burns and the corporations have 'framed up' a case on them."

Chandler was afraid that Harriman, as mayor, would work on behalf of the unions and kill the *Times'* open-shop policy. Historian Carey McWilliams noted that Harriman's election would also have been a blow to the plans for the aqueduct. As a candidate, Harriman was already attacking the use of public bond money to transport Owens Valley's water for the benefit of land developers in Los Angeles. The sale of the aqueduct bonds wasn't going well. Only $17 million of the $23 million in bonds to finance its construction had been sold. As major investors in the Los Angeles Suburban Homes Company, Otis, Chandler, and their partners needed Owens Valley water to develop San Fernando Valley land. Clearly, for Harry Chandler, the great dealmaker, the time to make a deal with his enemies was now—before the trial began.

Negotiating a Plea Bargain

Darrow, who believed the McNamara brothers to be guilty, proposed a plea bargain to save them from hanging. His ally was the well-known muckraking journalist Lincoln Steffens, who feared the trial would divide the city and hurt the liberal-union cause. They proposed that Jim McNamara, the dynamiter, would plead guilty but be spared

General Otis (seated at right) and his cohorts share a somber moment after the bombing. OPPOSITE: John J. "J.J." McNamara and his brother Jim in San Quentin. Jim spent the rest of his life there, but J.J. was released after serving ten years. Both men died in 1941.

the death penalty, while charges would be dropped against his older brother, John, who was accused of initiating and financing the plot.

Steffens and Darrow knew they needed General Otis and Harry Chandler to support the deal. Steffens typed out the terms, which were delivered to Chandler by an intermediary. Days of intense negotiation followed. "General Otis, as expected, became furious at the plan," Harry Chandler said. "He stormed about declaring, 'I want those sons-of-bitches to hang!' It was some time before he could be placated by the argument that it would be much better for his own cause if the trial were ended this way." In his autobiography, Steffens described the interaction between the general and his son-in-law. He said Otis had been alerted to the deal by a telegram from a construction-industry trade group, which insisted on the maximum penalty. Steffens was meeting with Chandler when "I saw General Otis marching menacingly at us with a telegram waving in his hand. He paid no attention to me. 'Harry,' he called, still coming, 'what is this, Harry?' Harry Chandler came like a bad little boy out of his office."

The general finally supported the deal but the district attorney wouldn't go along. On December 1, 1911, the brothers pleaded guilty. James McNamara was sentenced to life in prison. John McNamara received fifteen years instead of the freedom Darrow had proposed. In the mayoral election, Harriman was defeated. The guilty pleas destroyed the spirit of the labor movement in Los Angeles, and the city remained a bastion of the open shop for the next quarter of a century.

In a footnote to the affair, one member of the McNamara team, Joseph Scott, won a satisfying victory. After the trial, Otis had continued to attack Scott, who was up for re-election to the school board. Otis, his vehemence undiminished by advancing age, wrote: "The disgrace to Los Angeles is that Joseph Scott, of this dynamite-murder defense trio, is still a member of the Board of Education." Scott said, "He never let up on me. He pilloried me during the four days between the end of the trial and my candidacy for re-election . . . when I managed to be re-elected but by a diminished vote. From that time until I retired from the school board in 1915, he took every occasion to vilify me in the *Times*." Scott saved those vilifications, gathering material for a libel suit. He eventually won his case before the California Supreme Court, which upheld a lower court verdict awarding Scott $47,549.71.

In the final years of his life, perhaps influenced by memories of the dead and wounded he saw in the Civil and Spanish-American Wars, General Otis called for an alliance of nations dedicated to ending global conflicts, something that had long been discussed by international legal scholars and peace activists. It was surprising that support for the proposal came from such a warrior of a man. For, in terms of history, Harrison Gray Otis was defined by warfare—political and verbal—against his many enemies.

Most of his enemies had been driven from the field by the time the general died in 1917. Los Angeles was his, from the harbor to the northern reaches of the San Fernando Valley, prosperous and free of the unions he hated. "A few days before the general died . . . [his grandson] Norman drove him around Van Nuys and the valley," said Otis Booth. "He wanted to see the land."

After Gen. Harrison Gray Otis's death on July 30, 1917, the family had intended for his funeral to be held at the home of his daughter Marian and her husband, Harry Chandler. But so many wanted to attend that the service was moved to the First Congregational Church in downtown Los Angeles. A military burial for the old soldier at Hollywood Cemetery was arranged by the Grand Army of the Republic.

The *Times* ballyhooed Los Angeles as "the white spot" of America—a city free of crime, corruption, communism, and, by implication, non-white races.

Journalism as the objective pursuit of news or journalists as monitors of the community were things Harry Chandler never heard of.

"In the bonanza years from 1920 to 1930, Los Angeles had all the giddiness, the parvenu showiness and the crazy prosperity of a gold rush town."   —Carey McWilliams

"I think of Harry Chandler not as a publisher but as a land developer, a dreamer, a builder. His mind wasn't on the newspaper, I hate to tell you."   —Dorothy Chandler

"THERE ISN'T A PUBLIC OFFICE IN THE WORLD I WOULD WANT TO ACCEPT AS A RESULT OF MY MANY YEARS OF WORK AT THE *TIMES* OFFICE. I'M ABLE TO RENDER A SERVICE TO THE PUBLIC THAT IS FAR BEYOND ANYTHING I COULD IN ANY ELECTED POSITION."

—HARRY CHANDLER

CHAPTER THREE

Harry Chandler: The Empire Builder

In the early days, Harry Chandler and his family lived on a hill a short distance from the paper, making it easy for him to walk to the *Times* after dinner, when he welcomed people to his office. By 1914 he was rich enough to begin construction of an estate in Los Feliz, a fashionable neighborhood several miles northwest of downtown at the edge of the city's large Griffith Park. The same year, Cecil B. DeMille bought a home in the area. Chandler's Georgian-style house, with an unobstructed view of the park on one side and his growing city on the other, had twenty-four rooms, including eight bedrooms, four bathrooms, and a one-bedroom guest house. Although no longer within walking distance of the *Times*, he continued his nocturnal office hours.

From a lookout point in the Santa Monica Mountains, Harry views his land holdings in the San Fernando Valley. PAGES 62-63: Downtown Los Angeles in the 1920s was a lively place, becoming a sophisticated metropolis. The city's banks line busy Spring Street. PAGES 64-65: The old *Times* newsroom where reporters wore coats and ties and the copy editors wore green eyeshades. Stories were sent to the composing room by pneumatic tubes, and the news came out just the way Harry Chandler liked it. PAGES 66-67: Harry (center runner) hoofing it in a footrace at the 1910 *Los Angeles Times* annual picnic. Footraces were especially popular at outdoor events. PAGE 68: Harry at home, playing a game of dominoes with his wife Marian. PAGE 69: Harry's hobbies were gardening and maintaining a cow and beehives for his favorite drink: milk and honey.

HARRY'S SUPPLICANTS

When Harry Chandler returned to the paper each evening, a room of supplicants waited outside his office. "They would wander in knowing that he was going to come down or he had talked to them that day, and he'd say, 'Well, you come in at nine and we'll talk it over' or 'you come it at ten and we'll talk it over,'" recalled his son Norman. In middle age, Harry was like an old political boss or godfather, all-powerful in his Southern California world.

Some of Chandler's visitors were looking for a handout, and he sometimes obliged. "He had a very soft heart," Norman remembered. "Some woman would come in and give him a sob story and he'd listen and maybe advance her a little money, never expecting to get it back." Norman's wife Dorothy added, "And yet when it came to his own family, generosity was not a thing that was close to Harry Chandler or part of his character."

Some of the visitors had business ideas worth pursuing. Los Angeles was full of opportunities for making money. Land development was no longer the only avenue to wealth. Oil, motion pictures, aviation, shipping, and motor vehicles all had great potential as the nation began a decade of comparative prosperity following World War I.

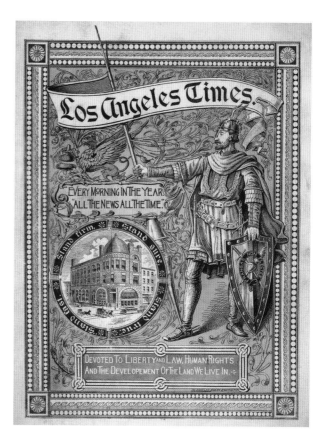

A MODERN LOS ANGELES

Modern Los Angeles was born in the 1920s, its progress reflected on the streets right outside the newspaper. Streetcars clattered past First Street and Broadway, site of the four-story newspaper building, which

The etched figure of a knight appeared on bound volumes of some *Times* publications. Harry Chandler, dressed in knight's armor, obligingly posed for this photograph. The costume may have been for a "fancy dress" party, fashionable in the 1920s.

resembled a fortress with a tower and rooftop battlements. The structure was General Otis's symbol of defiance, replacing the building that was bombed in 1910. Streets were crowded with cars. East on Broadway, department stores, office buildings, and movie theaters attested to the city's wealth, and Harry Chandler had a stake in many of these businesses. A few blocks away, the Pacific Electric Red Cars moved in and out of the terminal building on an interurban rail network that reached west to the beach and east through the San Gabriel Valley, past more Chandler property, and then on to the edge of the desert. Another line ran north into the San Fernando Valley, the first source of Chandler's real estate wealth.

Chandler's domain reached far beyond the Pacific Electric tracks. By the 1920s, his interests included huge ranches in Mexico, Colorado, and in the hills east of Los Angeles. He had stakes in an airline, oil wells, and aircraft manufacturing, as well as in the Ahwahnee Hotel in Yosemite National Park, a shipyard, and a steamship line. He was on more than fifty boards of directors. Much of his wealth was hidden in various corporations and trusts. The money he made was instrumental in providing venture capital for many enterprises, ranging from traditional land development to creative schemes conceived by scientific and industrial pioneers. These new ideas were well beyond anything previously imagined by General Otis and others in his generation of old-fashioned entrepreneurs.

In person, Chandler was a down-home mixture of business acumen, quirkiness, acquisitiveness, cheapness, stubbornness, ambition, and curiosity. As a youth, he'd been tall and handsome in a way that distinguished the men in the Chandler family. In his mature years, he was a white-haired, reserved man, who dressed in conservative suits that didn't fit him well. He had no patience for standing still while a tailor measured him. Nor did he want to sit to have shoes fitted. He shopped by phone, relying on measurements of an earlier version of his body.

Of all his attributes, his remarkable vision was the most important. Vision

A parade marches down Broadway toward the *Times* building. The paper heavily promoted civic events, such as this one, devoting plenty of news space to publicize them.

distinguished him from the other rich men who ran Los Angeles, especially when it came to Southern California's economy. The newspaper also gave him power over others. To him, the *Times* wasn't published to inform people or act as a civic watchdog. It was his personal megaphone, through which he delivered praise for his various business enterprises—and invectives for his enemies.

In 1920 when he and other members of the Los Angeles oligarchy started the California Company, an investment, stock underwriting, and banking firm, the *Times'* Chapin Hall, one of Chandler's most trusted reporters, wrote in the news columns that the company "will handle only securities of unquestioned investment character . . . and it is expected that many strong issues will be originated through this organization."

Even in those days—before newspapers and journalists became concerned with ethical conduct—Chandler's *Times* was noteworthy for the brazen way it promoted his business interests and the related cause of boosting Los Angeles. As his daughter-in-law Dorothy Buffum Chandler said:

> Harry Chandler just let other people run things. He was never really [involved in] the publishing, publisher sense. He was more interested in the community and land development, and things like that . . . I think of Harry Chandler as not a publisher but as a land developer, a dreamer, a builder. His mind wasn't on the newspaper . . . but he was on other things that have made Los Angeles as great as it is.

INFANT AVIATION INDUSTRY

Of all the visitors to Harry Chandler's office in 1920, none was of more lasting significance than aeronautical engineer, Donald Douglas.

Chandler's vision, combined with his curiosity, prompted an interest in the aircraft industry, which was struggling to fulfill the promise it had shown during World War I. Certainly the Southern California weather, permitting year-round flying, made the area a perfect fit. A few industry pioneers had built planes in Los Angeles, but they moved east as the federal government handed out wartime manufacturing contracts. With the war over, Chandler assigned one of his star reporters, Bill Henry, to check out the industry and see what it could offer Los Angeles. He gave Henry a year off to work with Glenn Martin, a Los Angeles aviation pioneer, who had shifted his operation to Cleveland. While studying Martin's operation, Henry met Douglas, who had a contract to build three planes for the Navy but lacked the money to begin the job.

Henry suggested Douglas come west and meet with Chandler. It was just a matter of squeezing Douglas in between the cronies, business associates, and supplicants who lined up to see the publisher during his office hours. Henry brought Douglas in and explained their mission to Chandler. The publisher listened and said, "I don't know much about either aviation or Mr.

OPPOSITE: Harry Chandler (second from left) and fellow passengers on a maiden flight of one of three Fokker F-10 tri-motor airplanes purchased by Western Air Express in May 1928. Chandler, an early champion of aviation, was one of the airline's investors.

"THERE IS ONE CITY IN THE UNITED STATES WHERE A STRIKE HAS NEVER BEEN ABLE TO SUCCEED. THAT CITY IS LOS ANGELES. THE REASON IS BECAUSE IT HAS THE *LOS ANGELES TIMES*." —HARRY CHANDLER

Douglas, Mr. Henry, but if you think they're both O.K. I'll help. How much do you need, Mr. Douglas?" Douglas replied, "Fifteen thousand dollars." Chandler wrote the names of nine Los Angeles businessmen on a piece of paper and a letter of introduction. He said if the nine would each guarantee a bank loan of fifteen hundred dollars, he would sign for the balance.

Douglas began making planes in Santa Monica, and the *Times* enthusiastically supported him. When the Navy selected his planes for a round-the-world flight in 1925, the *Times* ran a long article by Douglas under the headline, "Los Angeles Furnished Plan, Plane." That same year, the paper ran an editorial asking, "Which American city will be known as the 'aviation Detroit' and the creator of multimillionaire airplane builders? . . . Is there any reason why that city should not be Los Angeles?" And, when a group of German aeronautical experts visited the Douglas plant in 1927, the *Times* ran a story with the headlines, "German Air Delegation Astonished. Group Finds Fast Aviation Development in America; Douglas Plant Visited."

To encourage young men to go to work in aviation, the *Times* sponsored free Saturday courses at the National Aeronautical School near the University of Southern California campus, east of downtown. A story in the paper explained, "boys will receive the entire ground schooling that would help them in later years in the knowledge of aviation as this industry develops."

In 1924, Chandler was a member of the party that accompanied Dwight F. Davis, the secretary of war, on part of a tour of potential air bases, as was the paper's Washington correspondent Robert B. Armstrong, who was also Chandler's emissary to Washington's powerful. The secretary and his two daughters, in fact, spent a night at the Chandler Tejon ranch. Chandler, along with his realtor friend William Garland and James Talbot, head of Richfield Oil, also financed Western Air Express, which carried air mail on Douglas planes and later expanded to passenger service.

BRINGING THE PEOPLE

The Owens Valley water and the harbor made L.A.'s industrial growth possible, as did continuous promotional campaigns designed to persuade people to move there. The *Times'* Annual Midwinter Number was distributed around the country, sending a message of perpetual sunshine, affordable homes, and jobs. The January 1, 1925, issue featured a rugged, serious-looking man rolling up his sleeves to begin work on another aqueduct, this one to bring water from the Colorado River. Behind him was a rendering of the vast panorama of the Southland. The image conveyed a message of jobs not only on the water project but everywhere in Southern California. Another *Times* Annual Midwinter Number proclaimed:

> Southern California is the land of Eternal Springtime. It is the playground of America. The East wilts beneath the sweltering midsummer sun. Southern California knows not the meaning of a torrid summer. The East shivers in the cold embrace of wintry blizzards. Southern California knows not the frigidity of eastern winters.

OPPOSITE: Henry Huntington (back seat, left) in a motorcar with Harry Chandler visiting the Tejon Ranch. The *Los Angeles Times* and Huntington worked toward a common goal—developing Los Angeles.

Chandler and his business colleagues helped persuade tire-manufacturing companies and automakers to build plants in Los Angeles, offering to buy stock or provide other financial assistance. He got the potential investors together most famously at lunches at the paper or a club. Dorothy Chandler recalled, "He would say . . . I'll give one thousand dollars. What will you give? . . . and then everybody sitting around the table just had to follow suit with an equal amount or else they weren't asked to the next meeting, probably." Or, as the headline on a *Saturday Evening Post* profile of him said, "It costs one thousand dollars to have lunch with Harry Chandler."

THE NEXT STEP: OCEAN LINERS

He used the paper relentlessly to promote his enterprises. He, his friend Moses Sherman, and a few other business associates, along with his nephew Ralph Chandler, formed the Los Angeles Steamship Company to run steamers up the coast to San Francisco and across the Pacific to Hawaii. Robert Armstrong, Chandler's man in Washington, helped the company make cut-rate purchases of surplus transports from the federal government. Service to Hawaii began with a sendoff in the *Times* for the *City of Los Angeles*, a reconditioned German ship that had been seized during the war. "Glistening in her new coat of white," the paper

said, it sailed from the Los Angeles harbor "with one of the most notable passenger lists ever assembled on a steamer in the Pacific." When it brought its distinguished passengers back to Los Angeles, the *Times* reported that they "had a wonderful voyage. . . . The new steamer is now in effect a private yacht with all the comforts of a modern hotel and is declared by all to be the 'Queen of the Pacific,' the most comfortable and luxurious craft on the western sea."

ABOVE: Harry Chandler (third from right) and some colleagues at the Tejon Ranch. Harry and several partners purchased the property in 1912. It was his favorite retreat, and he often entertained business associates at the 270,000-acre spread. RIGHT: Along with other forms of transportation to bring newcomers to Los Angeles, Harry Chandler promoted train travel. He was also a motivating force behind the building of the elegant Union Station northeast of downtown Los Angeles.

Chandler did more than turn his news columns into advertisements for his steamship company. Another of his liners, the *City of Honolulu*, caught fire returning from Honolulu. The passengers were loaded on lifeboats provisioned with roast chicken and other food, drinks, and cigarettes, then put aboard an army transport returning troops home to San Francisco. A Chandler colleague on the boat heard that the San Francisco press—hostile to the Los Angeles line—would be waiting to interview the passengers and write stories mocking L.A.'s pretensions. Chandler fired off a message to the secretary of war, who ordered the troop ship to head to Los Angeles and a reception by friendlier reporters. The soldiers and sailors, whose families were awaiting them in San Francisco, were on the verge of mutiny.

SCIENTIFIC INFRASTRUCTURE

Chandler and colleagues such as Henry Huntington, who built the Pacific Electric interurban train network, knew the conversion to industry would require scientific expertise as well as the concrete and steel for the aqueduct, the harbor, and the railroad lines. Although the term wasn't in use at the time, what they envisioned was an economy based on advanced technology. Technology, in the form of Mulholland's engineering, had built the aqueduct. Engineering created the harbor. Technology would equip Los Angeles for the future.

In the mid-1920s, their attention turned to the California Institute of Technology in Pasadena. Caltech, committed to educating a small number of students in an atmosphere of scientific distinction, was not ranked among the top schools of its kind. Recognizing the need for scientists and engineers for the region, Chandler, Huntington, and other Southern California magnates raised the money that helped build Caltech into a world-renowned institution, instrumental in Southern California's industrial growth.

Caltech was where Donald Douglas would go in the 1930s when he developed his revolutionary passenger plane, the DC-1. Chandler and Douglas worked with Robert Millikan, who headed Caltech, in developing the Caltech wind tunnel, where the DC-1 was tested. A later version, the DC-3 initiated the era of mass-passenger flight.

By 1938, two years after the introduction of the DC-3, a quarter of the aircraft manufactured in the United States were built in the Los Angeles area. When the nation began arming for the impending World War II, Los Angeles, with its scientific infrastructure, airplane

An advertisement in the *Los Angeles Times* makes use of the "White Spot" slogan to promote a real-estate venture.

INVEST in the "White Spot"

The Greatest Development Los Angeles Has Ever Known Is Occurring In and Around Bandini NOW!

FACTS:

Harry Chandler in downtown Los Angeles. The white building at left is the county building, where Harry controlled yet another layer of government.

factories, and year-round good weather, combined with a large number of skilled and semi-skilled workers, became the center of the nation's aircraft industry. After the war, Southern California continued to dominate aerospace.

L.A. OF THE 1920s

Promising as it may have been for the future, aviation technology failed to catch the imagination of many Angelenos in the 1920s. The relentless promotion by Chandler and other boosters had brought in huge numbers of people, and the population of Los Angeles County—the city and adjacent areas—was on its way to more than doubling from 936,455 in 1920 to 2,208,492 in 1930. General Otis had been clear on the kind of immigrant he wanted:

> Los Angeles wants no dudes, loafers and paupers; people who have no means who trust to luck, cheap politicians, bummers, scrubs, impecunious clerks . . . We need workers! Hustlers! Men of brains, brawn and guts! Men who have a little capital and a good deal of energy—first class men.

The mix of immigrants, however, included many who were just what the general did not want—dudes, loafers, paupers, losers hoping for a break, all drawn to the western edge of the continent by a vague hope of a better life. Disappointment awaited many of them. And failure in the new land, far from home, was worse without the support of family, friends and familiar surroundings. After coming so far, and landing in a place so different than their Midwestern and Eastern homes, these new Californians were eager to find comfort from glib, glamorous evangelists, or doctors—fake and real—peddling their nostrums. Los Angeles in the 1920s became a city of salesmen, followers, and founders of cult religions and purveyors of strange health and rejuvenation fads and, of course, dreams. The most compelling dream—one that has been part of California since the Gold Rush—was that of striking it big. In the 1920s, oil was the new gold.

A promotional photo illustrating Southern California's mild weather and its residents' love of fitness. The sea of white faces and pale bodies also served as a reminder to prospective residents that the area was "the white spot" boosted by the *Los Angeles Times.*

City Made for the Automobile

There was plenty of demand for oil. The climate that made Southern California so attractive to airplane manufacturers also was perfect for the automobile. More than any other place in the world, Los Angeles became the city of the automobile. Cars could carry Southern Californians to the mountains or the beach with the mobility and privacy that the Pacific Electric Red Cars could not match. The auto quickly developed its own culture of drive-in restaurants, long commutes, and freedom to roam. Sexual freedom expanded, at least to a degree, and a car became a status symbol as well as a necessity. The car culture, and the distant residential suburbs it permitted, would eventually spread throughout the United States, particularly after World War II. But it all began in Los Angeles.

Horses were still attached to plows, but the San Fernando Valley had begun its love affair with the automobile.

Chandler, attuned to the importance of transportation to the development of his sprawling domain, was an early financial backer of L.A.'s auto and tire factories, as well as oil ventures. He invested in the Goodyear Tire and Rubber Co. when it built plants in Los Angeles, and he backed prospecting companies looking for oil in the Los Angeles basin. Tall drilling towers became part of the landscape, feeding the enormous appetite for oil. So many people were driving cars that on July 20, 1920, the *Times* reported a fuel shortage in Los Angeles. Trainloads of gasoline came from Texas, Oklahoma, and Kansas to supply the motorists. A service station in Hollywood, owned by Puente Oil, a Chandler company, usually reserved its fuel for film industry vehicles. But faced with the crisis, the station opened its pumps to all motorists once the movie trucks were filled. The narrow winding road through the Cahuenga Pass into the San Fernando Valley was becoming one of the most heavily traveled and congested roads in Southern California.

Oil, the automobile, and real estate were intertwined, and Harry Chandler and the city profited from it all. He made money from the sale of cars, tires, and gas to motorists shopping for homes of their own. When they reached the San Fernando

In an early use of telemarketing, every Angeleno with telephone service was called with an invitation to an opening day barbeque when the Los Angeles Suburban Homes Company began selling lots in 1911. Trains and cars brought prospective buyers to the barren site called Van Nuys, which was hailed in the *Times* as one of the "Wonder Towns of the San Fernando Valley." OPPOSITE: A rare shot of the opening of the Los Angeles Aqueduct on November 5, 1913, as the water arrived in Los Angeles. The photographer climbed the hill next to the flowing water and took the photo from the top of the cascades, looking south. The area was Owensmouth (later Canoga Park), owned by a syndicate of investors including Harry Chandler.

Valley floor, they headed to towns and subdivisions on land owned by Chandler and his partners. The subdivisions at first were just promoters' dreams or, at best, dots on a map. But Chandler's Los Angeles Suburban Homes Co. and San Fernando Mission Land Co. were about to pay off. One Chandler-built development was named Van Nuys, after Harry Chandler's friend and business associate Isaac Van Nuys. Marian was another, named for Chandler's wife, who was also General Otis's daughter. Otis dubbed the third housing tract Owensmouth, a name inspired by the fresh water coming from the Owens Valley. Marian eventually became Reseda and Owensmouth became Canoga Park.

Through its news columns, the *Times* worked to assure the enterprise's success. Author Kevin Roderick wrote, "before a single board was nailed, the *Times*, doing its part to sell the boss's lands, proclaimed the nonexistent new communities 'the Wonder Towns' of the San Fernando Valley." A road connecting the prospective towns was described as a "masterwork of civil engineering . . . that ranks with the best hard-surfaced roads in the world." An advertisement in the *Times* for another subdivision still on the drawing boards, Holly Heights, warned, "Everybody desires to own his own home and most everybody desires to live in Southern California . . . In and about Los Angeles desirable home sites are being 'gobbled up.'" After General Otis died in 1917, five hundred and fifty of his valley acres were sold for one hundred and twenty-five thousand dollars to Edgar Rice Burroughs, the best-selling author of the *Tarzan* books. He subdivided the land and called it Tarzana.

OIL FEVER

Oil shares and property that might be atop oil fields were sold with as much splash as the San Fernando Valley real estate. One developer called his subdivision, near an oil field, Petroleum Gardens. A flyer urged people to "buy where BIG DEVELOPMENTS are coming . . . All OIL and MINERAL RIGHTS go with each lot." Speculators brought busloads of potential customers to such places. So wild was oil fever that the City of Long Beach debated whether to abandon its central business district and turn it into an oil field. In the transient, ever-changing Los Angeles society, new promoters were accepted at face value.

So it was not unusual that 1920s Los Angeles welcomed C.C. Julian, a Texas oil field worker who drifted into California in the early days of the boom, broke but eager to speculate. He managed to pull together enough money to buy oil leases and persuade overly eager Los Angeles residents to buy stock in his Julian Petroleum Company. He seemed to understand how to reach them, with folksy radio advertisements on KMTR, directed at people who had left family and friends behind. It was the same approach used by the phenomenally successful Los Angeles evangelist, Aimee Semple McPherson, who drew thousands to her Angelus Temple. "Folks, I'm calling on you," Julian said in one ad, "yes and I'm calling like no human being ever called before."

OPPOSITE: Signal Hill, near Long Beach, studded with oil well towers. Shell Oil discovered oil here in June 1921. That first gusher, revealing the oilfield as one of the richest in the world, changed Signal Hill's history. The area became known as "oil town."

Harry Chandler didn't invest with Julian, although many of his rich friends did. But the *Times* accepted thousands of dollars for Julian's flow of newspaper ads. Before the Julian enterprise collapsed and he fled the state, forty thousand people handed him eleven million dollars in investments. It began to come apart when the California state corporations commissioner, Edward Michael Daugherty, investigated Julian and denied him a business permit. Daugherty had been a *Times* reporter and remained close to Chandler. Julian went to Chandler and asked him to intervene with Daugherty. Julian later insisted that Chandler had agreed to do this. But the morning after he'd met with Chandler, Julian saw Daugherty, who told him that even if he—Julian— lived to be ninety, he'd never get the permit.

Julian blamed Chandler and the *Times* for his own mounting legal and financial problems. He took his attack to the radio on June 20, 1927, but the hour-long broadcast was inaudible, constantly interrupted by whistles and static. He said the *Times*-owned KHJ had deliberately used its powerful transmitter to block the KMTR signal. What was interesting about the incident was the public's reaction. Despite the *Times*' stories attacking Julian, the stock price of Julian's enterprise temporarily increased. When he accused Chandler of jamming his broadcast, thousands sent telegrams denouncing the *Times*. It was yet another indication that not everyone lured west by Chandler's paper held him in high regard.

HOLLYWOODLAND

While oil, manufacturing, and land provided the muscle for Los Angeles's growth, the industry that gave L.A. its gloss and image was motion pictures. Filmmakers' culture and economics were foreign to Chandler. He invested only a little in the business and preferred Hollywood real estate to films. In 1923, he, his friend Moses Sherman, and filmmaker Mack Sennett put up a big "Hollywoodland" sign to advertise their new subdivision. The "land" portion disappeared in 1949, and it is now the famous Hollywood Sign.

Chandler started a movie page in the *Times* called "Preview," which grew into a Sunday section. He also persuaded a number of filmmakers to move from foggy San Francisco to sunny Los Angeles. His paper added a Hollywood gossip columnist, Stella the Stargazer.

Even so, he remained ambivalent about the film business. Dennis McDougal wrote:

Neither Harry or Marian made a public fuss about their Congregationalist roots but the couple and their family were stern practitioners of biblical moderation, and the excesses that were built in to Hollywood's culture genuinely shocked and appalled them both. Little by little, the film colony's ongoing bacchanal pushed Chandler and his *Times* toward the brink of censorship. The *Times* dropped Stella the Stargazer in the mid-1920s rather than celebrate the profligate lifestyles of Hollywood's rich and famous.

OPPOSITE: By 1928, one hundred and fifty families were living in Hollywoodland, and more homes and lots were being sold in the residential area developed by Harry Chandler and his partners. "Only ten minutes from Hollywood's 'Great White Way,'" a *Times* story said.

CRIMINAL SYNDICALISM ACT

Despite his expansive vision and willingness to try new business ventures, Harry Chandler followed the same hard line with labor that General Otis had established. From the time of Otis's death in 1917, when Chandler became publisher of the *Times*, he did everything in his power to make sure the unions were kept far away from his paper. It was true that the bombing of the *Times* and its aftermath had greatly weakened the labor movement in Los Angeles, but he worried about what he saw happening elsewhere in California and around the country. Nationally, the union threat had increased as a polarized America reacted sharply to World War I. Americans were changing, embracing new clothing styles, music, literature, and, despite the threat of prohibition, continuing their thirst for liquor, wine, and beer. They were also more open to new ways of doing things, such as union representation for workers and collective bargaining.

James E. Davis, Los Angeles police chief between 1926 and 1938, told his officers to "hold court on gunmen on the Los Angeles streets and I want them brought in dead." His "Red Squad" broke up union meetings, strikes, and anything the city's leaders considered radical. Meanwhile, his own department was riddled with corruption.

Chandler's pro-business organizations sensed that the tide might be turning against them. They got the state legislature and the governor to approve the Criminal Syndicalism Act of 1919. The law made it a felony to "advocate or promote violence to accomplish a change in industrial ownership or control or effecting any political changes." The penalty was one to fourteen years in prison. Violent action wasn't required for arrest; simply belonging to an organization that advocated violence was enough.

In Los Angeles, the police department vigorously enforced the act, and the alliance between the *Times* and the police tightened. The department formed a "Red Squad" to stop meetings, picketing, and other union and liberal demonstrations. The squad was so closely tied to the Chandler-led business community that at one point its office was in the Chamber of Commerce building.

The Red Squad, led by Captain William "Red" Hynes, left a lasting legacy. Under a variety of names, it continued into the late twentieth century. It set a pattern for the entire Los Angeles Police Department in dealing with dissent, not only among liberals but also with community organizers who challenged the LAPD's rough methods of enforcing the law in African American and Hispanic neighborhoods. Among the legacies of this kind of law enforcement were the Watts Riots of 1965 and the Los Angeles Riots of 1992.

The International Workers of the World, the I.W.W., known as the "Wobblies," was the prime leader of the leftist movement in the early twentieth century. In 1923, the I.W.W. called a strike in the Los Angeles harbor demanding higher wages and better working conditions for the maritime unions and a repeal of the Criminal Syndicalism Act. In a few days, ninety ships were marooned in the harbor. The Chamber of Commerce and the Merchants and Manufacturers Association demanded that the Los Angeles Police Department enforce the act and arrest the strikers. More than five thousand strikers and union supporters attended a Sunday rally in an area near the harbor known as Liberty Hill. Within two days, the police had arrested more than a thousand. After that, a famous I.W.W. supporter, novelist Upton Sinclair, spoke at Liberty Hill. All he did was recite the Bill of Rights, but it was enough to get him arrested under the police department's broad interpretation of the law.

ENTER UPTON SINCLAIR

Sinclair, a Socialist, was the author of *The Jungle*, a 1906 muckraking novel exposing filthy and inhumane conditions in the meat packing industry. In 1916, he and his wife Mary Craig Kimbrough moved to California, settling in Pasadena. Soon after he arrived, he spoke in meetings around the city and attracted the attention of Otis, still eager for a fight in his last year of life. After Sinclair's speech to the women of the Friday Morning Club, Otis wrote in an editorial that Sinclair was "an effeminate young man with a fatuous smile, a weak chin and a sloping forehead talking in a false treble." He also said the writer was a "slim beflanneled example of perverted masculinity."

From his first days in town, Upton Sinclair, the muckraking author of the *The Jungle*, despised General Harrison Gray Otis. The feeling was mutual, bringing out both men's most colorful vitriol.

Sinclair later had his say in his book of journalism criticism, *The Brass Check: A Study in American Journalism*: "I have lived in Southern California four years and it is literally a fact that I have yet to meet a single person who does not despise and hate his *Times* . . . This paper, founded by Harrison Gray Otis, one of the most corrupt and most violent old men that ever appeared in American public life, has continued for thirty years to rave at every conceivable social reform, with complete disregard for the truth, and with abusiveness which seems almost insane."

Sinclair helped found the American Civil Liberties Union in California in 1923 and ran for governor in 1926 and 1930 as a Socialist, receiving about fifty thousand votes each time. In 1933, when California was deep in the Depression, he changed his registration to Democratic and wrote a pamphlet, "I, Governor of California, and How I Ended Poverty." He then announced his candidacy for the Democratic nomination for governor. End Poverty in California—EPIC—was his slogan. It resonated in a state where the promise of the good life had been so cruelly shattered.

With EPIC, he proposed the state rent idle factories and put the unemployed to

In 1934, Upton Sinclair was the Democratic nominee for governor, running on a utopian platform he called "End Poverty In California" or EPIC. Here, he prepares to speak to a large audience in Inglewood, one of the working-class and middle-class communities where he was popular.

work in them. They would own the goods they produced. Farmers would bring their produce to state warehouses and receive vouchers, which could be used to pay their unpaid taxes. The factory workers would get their food from the warehouses in return for the goods they produced. The goods would be shipped to the farmers who could buy or barter them in exchange for produce. The EPIC plan also envisioned colonies where the state would rent unused land, provide machinery, and let the unemployed "grow their own food, making gardens where there are now patches of weeds."

There is no doubt that the Depression changed Harry Chandler's Los Angeles and the rest of California. A quarter of the state's population was living on public relief or private charity, and Chandler was completely out of touch with them. A *Times* editorial declared, "Much of the Depression is psychological."

The miseries of the Depression boosted an increase in Democratic registration. Democrats, who had been outnumbered by Republicans four-to-one before the previous state election, caught up with them. Aside from the bad economy, the state's Democratic gains were helped by Franklin D. Roosevelt's presidential victory in 1932 and a registration drive by a grassroots Sinclair

campaign anchored in hundreds of EPIC clubs throughout the state. A half-million Californians received an eight-page tabloid, the *EPIC News*, each week. A million of Sinclair's EPIC pamphlets were sold, providing money for the campaign. Sinclair won the Democratic nomination, receiving almost ninety thousand more votes in the primary election than the Republican governor, Frank F. Merriam. In Los Angeles County, EPIC candidates swept primary races for lower offices. Voters in the newly impoverished Los Angeles seemed to share Sinclair's contempt for the *Times*.

In the fall general election campaign, Chandler and his paper mobilized against Sinclair. A *Times* editorial warned that Sinclair's "maggot-like horde of Reds," were "termites secretly and darkly eating into the foundations and the roof beams of everything that the American heart has held dear and sacred."

But even the *Times* could see that the old bellowing and vitriol was out of style. Another approach was needed for an electorate that now got its information from radio and newsreels. Chandler had just the man: Kyle Palmer, the political editor.

ANOINTING A POLITICAL EDITOR

In the twenty-first century, with newspaper influence diminished, it is difficult to conceive of how a single journalist could accumulate enough power to be called "the little governor," "Mr. Republican," or "the kingmaker," as Palmer was. There was no television. California, then as now, had weak political parties with no bosses to put together slates of candidates. It was up to newspapers to fill the void.

Palmer shared Chandler's hatred of unions and liberals. He understood the twists and turns of politics better than businessman Chandler and was able to guide his boss through the more complex society that California was becoming. There were other powerful political editors in the state, particularly at the *Times'* conservative allies, the *San Francisco Chronicle* and the *Oakland Tribune*. As was the case with Palmer, the other top political editors were ambassadors for their publishers, as well as links to the political world. But no one had as much power as Palmer.

Chandler, busy with land development and other business deals, needed guidance. Politics was important to him. "He was interested in concentrating on the political activities and who he would support, and who he wouldn't support, and why, and the pros and cons," said his son Norman. "He devoted quite a bit of time to that." Dorothy Chandler recalled a trip to Washington when Chandler and Robert Armstrong, the paper's Washington correspondent, urged Herbert Hoover to run for president in 1928:

> I was in the next room and I just had the biggest ears because I was dying to hear what they were all saying. So I left a crack in the door so I could hear. Mr. [Harry] Chandler gave a great deal of leeway and responsibility to Kyle. He was kind of the political czar of the *Times*. And Mr. Chandler just let him go ahead in playing that role. He was very close to the top politicians, especially from California . . . And he was a very manipulating kind of a man in politics. I came to not like Kyle Palmer myself because I do not like that kind of political behind-the-scenes activity . . . In those days the *Times* took his word for everything political, their stand on everything. I did not like it.

Politicians were respectful and sometimes fearful when they came to see "the little governor," Kyle Palmer. Palmer was largely responsible for picking the candidates the paper would support. One thing was certain: they would be Republicans.

Palmer may have been powerful in the political world, but in the Chandler hierarchy, he was just an employee, albeit a top hand. Dorothy Chandler said:

> He had no sense of money . . . He was very extravagant. He built a house up near the Greek Theater, up there in the hills, quite attractive. And he was living up there with his third wife. He was loaned the money to build the house by Mr. [Harry] Chandler . . . Kyle was . . . supposed to pay [the loan] back slowly to Mr. Chandler, [but] he got way behind in his payments. Mr. Harry Chandler felt sorry for Norman and me because we were living in this apartment down on Vermont. My daughter . . . just had been born. So he said, "until Kyle can give us some payments, I'll give you the house. And you just go and live there and pay the same rent you would've paid at the apartment. So we did." We had a very happy couple of years there before Kyle did pay some money back, and we had to get out. We built a house nearby ourselves.

ANTI-SINCLAIR CAMPAIGN

In the campaign against Sinclair and EPIC, Palmer directed the *Times* coverage, wrote anti-Sinclair editorials, and raised money and wrote speeches for Republican Gov. Frank Merriam. Film studio owners and executives, especially Louis B. Mayer, hated Sinclair as much as Chandler did. So Palmer also worked on the movie industry's campaign against the Democratic nominee.

Palmer understood the technology of politics and was a spark plug for a campaign that would be remembered for giving birth to modern media politics. Historian Greg Mitchell wrote, "The 1934 governor's race in California showed candidates the way from the smoke-filled rooms to Madison Avenue. Media experts, making unprecedented use of film, radio, direct mail, opinion polls, and national fundraising devised the most astonishing (and visually clever) smear campaign ever directed against a major candidate."

Sinclair lost to Governor Merriam, and Palmer's influence increased. He saw that the Republicans had to change if they were to keep control of the governor's office. The Democrats won in 1938, but the canny Palmer came up with a winner four years later, Earl Warren, the attorney general who was pro-business but sympathetic to social legislation and willing to sit down with labor. Harry Chandler didn't like such policies, nor did Palmer. "He was horrified at some of the proposals of Mr. Franklin D. Roosevelt," Norman Chandler said of his father. "He thought [FDR] was going to spend so much money that the country was going absolutely busted." But he did like Warren. Everybody did. Harry and his friends knew the new governor could keep the state Republican during the Roosevelt years.

Harry Chandler looks at a headline in the *Olvera Street News* celebrating his birthday. Chandler was responsible for the creation of the popular tourist attraction, located on the northern edge of downtown Los Angeles.

HARRY HAS THE RECORDS BURNED

Harry Chandler died of coronary thrombosis in 1944 at the age of eighty. He had made history, but he didn't want anyone to know how he did it. By his order, all his business and personal files were burned. The business correspondence, notes, contracts, and other records of how he built the city, the newspaper, and an incalculable fortune were lost to history. But Harry Chandler, like the smartest of the old political bosses, probably didn't put everything in writing, not when business could be done by a nod or a handshake.

Of all his ideas, none had more lasting importance to the Los Angeles area than his understanding that science—aeronautics in particular—would be the engine of the Southland's growth. He promoted it in his newspaper, raised money for Caltech, and persuaded and bullied his business colleagues into investing their wealth in aerospace enterprises that became the backbone of the Southern California economy. Caltech's Jet Propulsion Laboratory, established in the 1930s, is a world pioneer and leader in space exploration. From Lockheed-Martin at the edge of the Mojave Desert to plants along the coast, the aerospace industry survives, reduced but still vital.

His political legacy was already disappearing at the time of his death. His last candidate for governor, Earl Warren, was too liberal for Harry. Warren favored government health insurance and other social programs, and sat down in a friendly manner with union leaders. Roosevelt's New Deal had given unions new power to organize, and Chandler's Criminal Syndicalism Act was a little-remembered relic of the past. Workers in the aircraft, auto and tire plants, and shipyards he had brought to Southern California were union members. Kyle Palmer soldiered on and would still be Mr. Republican for a few more elections, but his influence through the *Times* would wane. A new publisher, Norman Chandler, was in charge and he would begin to run the paper in a different way.

During the post-war baby boom generation, the population of Los Angeles County exploded—from three to six-and-a-half million people.

In keeping with family tradition, the *Times* editorial policy under Norman Chandler remained pro-business, anti-union, and staunchly Republican.

"Norman Chandler said to me, 'Tom, you should know that this is a company that because of the trust and the way in which the company is structured will never be sold.'"
—Tom Johnson

In a 1964 cover story, *Time* magazine hailed Dorothy Chandler's efforts to build a downtown music center as "perhaps the most impressive display of virtuoso money-raising in the history of U.S. womanhood."

IT'S A TYPICALLY AMERICAN STORY FOR THE THIRD GENERATION TO RUN THE FAMILY BUSINESS INTO RUIN. BUT HARRY CHANDLER'S ELDEST SON NORMAN WOULD BUILD UPON WHAT HIS FATHER AND GRANDFATHER HAD CREATED.

CHAPTER FOUR

Norman Chandler: The Businessman

Norman Chandler was a different kind of publisher for the *Los Angeles Times*. He didn't have the bombast, anger, or vision of the first publisher, his grandfather, General Harrison Gray Otis. He lacked the cunning, ambition, acquisitiveness, and political instincts of his father, Harry Chandler. A self-effacing man, he paid particular attention to the opinions of his wife, Buff. Although she didn't have Otis or Chandler blood, she possessed a bit of the general's anger and determination and Harry's vision and political sense, all of which she would one day use to raise money for the Music Center in downtown Los Angeles. But while Buff got more notice, it was Norman who saved the financially shaky newspaper, diversified, and started the Times Mirror Co. on the road to becoming a media giant.

Norman Chandler sitting for a *Time* magazine cover portrait. PAGES 96-97: WPA artists in the 1930s created this scale model to help planners visualize downtown Los Angeles. PAGE 98: In the 1940s, the look of the newsroom hadn't changed much except for its configuration. Here, the head copy editor (center) was called "the dealer," and the assistant copy editors worked on "the rim." PAGE 99: In this 1949 shot, a *Times* photographer and reporter discussed an assignment with their editor. PAGE 100: Norman Chandler standing in front of the Mirror Building, part of the Times Mirror complex. PAGE 101: Norman relaxing on the family's seven-acre spread, "*Los Tiempos*" ("the Times"), in the San Gabriel Valley town of Santa Anita. PAGE 102: Dorothy "Buff" Chandler (at right) networking with the city's high society on behalf of the Music Center. PAGE 103: For charm and popularity, few couples could match Buff and Norman.

The Chandlers loved the outdoor life on their Tejon Ranch, as well as on their property in the San Gabriel Valley and elsewhere. Here, Norman Chandler gets exposure to ranch life at an early age.

During Norman's years as publisher, he was also a builder in the Chandler tradition and, like his father, used *Times* editorials and one-sided news stories to promote his favorite projects. These affected life in Los Angeles for many decades. The *Times*' power came from more than the printed page. The *Times* dominated Los Angeles City Hall, helped by an influential reporter who signaled thumbs up and thumbs down when telling council members how to vote on measures that interested the paper. The *Times* was the leading voice in state Republican politics and had clout in the legislature. It was hard to beat a combination like that.

Smog control is one example. As Norman told it in a joint interview, he and Buff were driving into Los Angeles from their home in Sierra Madre in 1946. As they came over the hill near Elysian Park, they saw the basin blanketed with a brown layer of smog. "I was goaded by Mrs. Chandler," he said "to the effect of why don't we do something about this." Buff, who enjoyed being the star, remembered it a bit differently. She said that she was driving alone when she saw the pollution. "So I just went into the office and I said to Norman, 'something has to be done,'" she said. "You said it sitting next to me in the car," Norman corrected her.

However the Chandlers were alerted, what followed was a great idea. Norman organized a citizens' committee and paid for a study of the smog problem by an eminent scientist. Chandler featured the scientist's report, which recommended countywide controls, in the paper. Then he and fellow businessmen in the Automobile Club of Southern California and the Los Angeles Chamber of Commerce got behind the recommendation. With *Times* editorial support, then-Governor Earl Warren signed legislation in 1947 authorizing smog control districts in every county. That created the Los Angeles Air Pollution District, the first of its kind in the nation and the beginning of present-day air pollution regulation.

Other Chandler projects were more traditional, reminiscent of the aqueduct and harbor of his forebears' days. As Chandler, describing past and future projects, put it in a *Times* Publisher's Opinion column in 1959,

> An improved airport, a great zoo, a union station, a superior baseball park, a sports arena, the redevelopment of Bunker Hill, a music center to become the core of music programs for all of Southern California, the freeways that will give us mobility, a rapid-transit system to knit our key centers together, the aqueducts that we must have—all the great components that we either have built or are preparing to build for all of Southern California—these are worth the kind of united effort that has changed our semi-desert into an amazing civilization within the short span of a hundred years.

RESCUING A SINKING ENTERPRISE

Norman Chandler moved into management as assistant general manager in the Depression year of 1936, taking over an economically strapped paper with an increasingly limited readership. As Buff—her name actually was Dorothy—recalled, "That was when my poor Norman got called into the fray. He had to pay the bills." Norman reversed a longstanding ban and the *Times* started accepting alcoholic-beverage ads. "It became obvious to me that [refusing such ads] was a silly policy to have, that more and more people were drinking socially . . . the big stores would run a full page selling all kinds of liquor . . . we were losing many hundreds of thousands of dollars a year just turning it down."

She said, "He did pull the *Times* out of its financial problems—he was a businessman's publisher." Or as Norman, lacking his wife's gift of dramatic description, put it, "The *Times* was not in very good shape financially so something had to give. I did have some ideas on how the paper was run . . . the lack of aggressive leadership." He eventually turned the limited Chandler family enterprise into the nation's largest newspaper company, raising many millions of dollars by going public—over the bitter opposition of other Chandler heirs. Although a thoroughly conservative Republican, he began to move the paper away from its one-sided political coverage. Norman ran the paper from 1941, when his father Harry retired, until 1960, when he handed the job of publisher over to his son, Otis. Until his retirement in 1968, Norman continued to guide the company's business expansion as chairman of the Times Mirror Co.

Not only were General Otis and Harry Chandler influential in the creation of the Los Angeles harbor, but the family owned a passenger steamship line. Here, the family checks out a steamer. From left: Helen Chandler, Marian Chandler, Constance Chandler, Philip Chandler, Dorothy Chandler, Harrison Chandler, and Norman Chandler.

Norman was likeable and quiet, a well-mannered man with more than his share of Chandler good looks. More importantly, he was the product of the rich, narrow Los Angeles society, composed to a large extent of men like him, heirs to fortunes accumulated by the moguls who had shaped Los Angeles. He went to Stanford, joined the right fraternity (Delta Kappa Epsilon), and was generally living the life his family expected of him when Buff, then a Stanford sorority girl, caught his eye. In an act of rebellion, he defied his mother and sisters, who opposed the match, to marry her in 1922.

BUFF'S ROLE IN THE FAMILY

The nickname *Buff* came from her maiden name, Buffum. Her family owned a chain of department stores based in Long Beach, and they were prominent in the civic and social affairs of the city. While her family may not have been as wealthy and prominent as the Chandlers, Buff was an heiress in her own right. Even so, few members of the Chandler family had shown up for the young couple's wedding. Marian Burke, longtime secretary to Buff, later said, "Well, they didn't think her father measured up . . . Buffum's was just dry goods stores in Long Beach. And that didn't measure up to what they got accustomed to." Buff herself said she didn't think her in-laws felt the Buffums fell short of the Chandler's social status. "[It] was not true that they felt he'd married below," she said. "That's fallacious."

Still, Buff's family relationships were a factor in the depression that struck her in 1932 after ten years of marriage. A friend recommended a psychiatrist in Pasadena, Dr. Josephine Jackson. She joined ten other patients in Jackson's house.

> I felt, during that year of depression . . . that I was a failure because I didn't go out to the garden club and the town club and play bridge . . . She made me feel that I had this important role in my life ahead of me with Norman . . . the role of the Chandler heritage . . . in Southern California, and that I had to be the one to help it to go forward to help him.

NORMAN'S STRENGTHS

Buff was a strong, charming woman who could also be domineering and argumentative. But Norman was clearly the boss. Their son, Otis Chandler, said:

> My father would say, "Darling you don't know what you're talking about, and I don't want to hear any more about it." So my father was not as dynamic as she is and not as forceful as she is but he is a very mellow person . . . and he was laid back . . .

This was power in Los Angeles. Harry (left) and Norman Chandler stand in the main entrance to the *Times* building. Although the personalities of father and son were different, they shared a vision of a big and booming Southland, and of their paper playing a major role in reaching that goal. OPPOSITE: Norman and Dorothy "Buff" Chandler made a handsome couple during their early years together.

But pushed too hard, Otis recalled, his father would tell Buff, "Relax. You don't know what you're talking about. I'll take care of it." Missy Chandler, Otis's first wife, said Norman was a peacemaker. She recalled an incident when she and Buff got into a shouting argument while the family was driving somewhere. "Norm said, 'Now girls, now girls, stop this. Buff, you be quiet. Missy, you be quiet. I don't want any more of this.'"

Norman was conservative. Otis said that when he succeeded his father "I was running too fast for him. He would have liked to have, I think, kept the paper a Republican paper and a conservative paper and he didn't like me putting black faces in the paper or Latino faces or running both sides of a labor-management dispute." His mother, on the other hand,

> was always excited when I was telling her all the things that we were going to do or that we were doing. She applauded that, whereas many times he didn't . . . She became, I think, much more liberal, if that's the right word. She became a liberal, I guess, in many areas, but he did not and I know sometimes when I was with them and they would be arguing between the two of them on some editorial position I'd had or something, . . . they would take quite different positions.

Norman was a companionable man who enjoyed a drink. Paul Conrad, the paper's Pulitzer Prize-winning cartoonist and a strong liberal, recalled an airplane flight with Norman Chandler. "We're the only ones in first class," Conrad said.

> I thought, what do I do now. Pretty soon, I get "Hey Paul, come on up. We can chat." So I did. We talked kind of all the way, I with my vodka, and he with his gin. I thought it was going to be the longest ride of my life, but he was just marvelous. Not putting me down, but suggesting where he wondered why in a particular situation why I'd go the way I went [in a cartoon]. So I'd explain it to him . . . He just flat out didn't understand liberals. I don't blame him; there are a whole lot of conservatives who don't understand liberals. But it was a real occasion, I swear. I never forgot that.

Taking on the Competition

In 1941, when Norman took over as publisher, the *Times* was trailing the competition. "The *Examiner* and *Herald* both passed us in circulation," Norman said. "The *Times* still held a slight lead in total advertising volume . . . [but] the *Times* was just coasting and coasting downhill." He hired an efficiency expert and "with his aid we did a lot of weeding out of deadwood." During the war, he struggled to find enough newsprint and made a crucial decision. Even though newsprint was short, he resolved to maintain the amount of space devoted to news and continue to try to increase circulation. "We started to gain and did gain on the *Herald* and then on the *Examiner,* and we got caught up with them and went by them, and they never had a chance to catch us again, circulation wise."

Even at its low point, the *Times* still held power over advertisers. Norman said:

> While not first in circulation, it was more prestigious in every respect. It had a better clientele of readers, people who had more purchasing power, far more purchasing power than the readers of the other papers. And that was why advertisers put the bulk of their money in the *Los Angeles Times*. It was a much more conservative newspaper in the presentation of the news than the other newspapers.

"I DID HAVE IDEAS AS TO HOW THE PAPER WAS RUN AND THE DEADWOOD
THAT WAS AROUND THERE—THE LACK OF AGGRESSIVE LEADERSHIP."
—NORMAN CHANDLER

PLEASING THE BASE

The news the *Times* presented and its emphasis on business-oriented growth was compatible with the beliefs, hopes, and prejudices of its subscribers. The paper's management saw nothing wrong with its slanted news coverage or editorials. But many of the growing Los Angeles middle class and working class—particularly ethnic minorities—were offended and angered.

One example of that disaffection involved the paper's coverage of the tangled story of Dodger Stadium.

The ballpark is located on the site of what was once a large barrio. Its destruction became a major event in the history of Latino Los Angeles. Originally, the Chavez Ravine barrio, by then owned by the city, was to be the site of public housing, a project supported by Mayor Fletcher Bowron. The *Times* opposed him for supporting public housing. As *Frontier Magazine* put it, "The *Times* reached out, gently tapped Congressman Norris Paulson on the shoulder and pointed to City Hall." Poulson won and in

the last three weeks of the election, the *Times* gave him 1,019 inches of space to 219 inches for Bowron. With the threat of public housing in Chavez Ravine gone, the *Times* favored turning the land over to the Brooklyn Dodgers, a team that wanted to move to Los Angeles. Many residents called it a giveaway, but with *Times* support, the plan was narrowly approved by the voters.

To Chandler and other business leaders, such coverage was a public service, promoting projects the city needed. The prestige advertisers—the high-end stores and auto agencies—no doubt loved it. So did the limited subscriber base, centered in WASP Pasadena, San Marino, Arcadia, Sierra Madre, and Hancock Park. The *Times* didn't bother these readers with pictures and stories of those they considered beneath their notice—Jews, Blacks, Latinos, Asians, or the poor in general—people who didn't fit into their restricted world. But more than a half-century later, the episode still stirs anger in the Latino community. The feelings were powerfully expressed in the play *Zoot Suit*, sentiments that continued to hurt the *Times* for years as it sought to build circulation in the growing Latino middle class. It did not, however, interfere with Latinos becoming a large part of the Dodger fan base.

If you wanted to sell a Cadillac or a fur coat, the *Los Angeles Times* was the place to advertise. From the 1920s into the 1970s, the *Times* cultivated a subscriber base in affluent Hancock Park, Pasadena, San Marino, and points east.

Outside the Latino community, a growing number of middle-class residents were put off by the stuffy, conservative *Times* and the way it ignored the city around it. They also didn't like its blind support for the baseball stadium and downtown redevelopment. They wanted lively news, sports, Hollywood, gossip, crime, and at least halfway-fair coverage of politics and government. What they didn't want was a paper that was boring as well as slanted. Other local papers attracted them. There was the *Examiner*, where City Editor Jim Richardson kept his aggressive staff in action; the *Herald Express*, where Aggie Underwood sent her crew chasing crime and celebrities; and the *Daily News*, the only paper that gave Democrats a fair shake.

ETHNIC UPHEAVAL OF THE 1940S

There is no better example of the paper's failure to cover the changing L.A. than its reporting of racial troubles during World War II. Take, for example, the way the paper handled the imprisonment of the West Coast's Japanese Americans and immigrant Japanese following the attack on Pearl Harbor. This sorry chapter in American history was approved by President Franklin D. Roosevelt and supported by California's Democratic and Republican political establishment, the state's newspapers, and the public. It followed years of anti-Asian agitation in California.

Although the *Times* wasn't substantially out of step with contemporary thought, its biased coverage was especially egregious given the key role the paper played as a leader of the community. The Japanese had been an important part of Los Angeles. In Boyle Heights, Roosevelt High School was notable for the way Japanese Americans, Latinos, Jews, and others mixed in classrooms and on athletic teams. But none of this appeared in the pages of the *Times* at the outbreak of the war. Instead, *Times* stories portrayed Japanese

Despite the happy faces in this picture, Mexican orchard and farm workers were not well treated in California. Their work involved long hours, low wages, and housing that was substandard, if provided at all. BOTTOM: A 1942 *Times* story reports the "voluntary" arrival of the first eighty-six Japanese Americans at Manzanar, the Owens Valley Reception Center. A total of thirty-five thousand evacuees, most of them American citizens, were interned at detention camps around the state.

California's long history of anti-Asian racism reached a new intensity after the Japanese bombed Pearl Harbor. Coverage by the *Times* and other papers fed suspicions that Japanese Americans were a danger to the country.

Americans as potential saboteurs.

From Washington, political editor Kyle Palmer wrote, somewhat illogically:

> The fact that there had been no sabotage showed Japanese Americans were obeying orders from Tokyo: Known plans of the Japanese military heads include instructions to Japanese in this country to observe the most loyal and circumspect attitude toward the United States until war developments reach a stage where sabotage can be made an active part of a military campaign.

In an editorial in January, 1942, the *Times* said, "The mounting wave of demands . . . that the federal government remove Japanese from military areas represents no sudden burst of hysteria . . . it is the calm, common-sense conclusion of patriotic citizens who are determined there shall be no Pearl Harbors here."

The treatment of other ethnic groups was equally poor. Since 1920, Mexicans had been the city's largest immigrant group from outside the country. They settled in Los Angeles, mostly on the Eastside, creating communities without the *Times* taking notice of them. Continuing to target white Midwestern immigrants, the paper advertised Los Angeles as the "white spot" of America—free of crime, corruption, and, communists and, by implication, non-white races. Professor Allison Varzally, a social, cultural and political historian at California State University, Fullerton, said, the *Times* wanted "Midwesterners who are looking for a place that is somewhat exotic and different in its weather and in the possibilities for constant leisure. But they also want a place that is familiar or at least has residents that look like their neighbors." Such pitches helped stimulate one of the nation's biggest internal migrations. During the 1920s, 1.5 million Americans moved to Southern California, a migration that grew during the Depression, World War II, and the years of postwar prosperity.

Over the years, the immigration became more diverse. The lure of California reached from working-class and impoverished Jews on New York's Eastside to Catholic immigrant neighborhoods in the East and Midwest; from black sharecroppers in the South to the Dust Bowl refugees immortalized by the songs of Woody Guthrie. As the 1940s began, this heterogeneous immigration grew as Americans were drawn to California by the wartime manufacturing that ended the Depression.

The *Times* didn't cover these newcomers, nor did the newcomers have much interest in reading the *Times*.

SLEEPY LAGOON

In the early years of World War II, the *Times*, along with the other newspapers, splashed stories of what they portrayed as an outbreak of Mexican youth-gang violence and supported the police and sheriff's deputies when they moved hard against young Mexican men.

The situation blew up in August 1942, when a young man was killed in a fight between Mexican American youths at a reservoir named Sleepy Lagoon, after a popular song. Within two days, police arrested more than six hundred people, most of them Mexican American boys and girls, as suspects in the killing. Seventeen boys were put on trial together. Twelve were convicted of murder in January 1943 and sent to San Quentin Prison. Liberals saw it as a racial issue, a sentiment that was strongly denied by the *Times*. A defense committee, with roots in the Jewish and Mexican American communities in Boyle Heights, was formed, with support from liberal elements in Hollywood. It blamed racist police, prosecutors, and courts. The formation of the Sleepy Lagoon Defense Committee was an important step in the early development of a civil rights movement in Los Angeles. Its efforts culminated in a reversal of the young men's convictions and their release.

"That this case was prosecuted in good faith there seems no reason whatever to doubt," the *Times* said in an October 7, 1944, editorial questioning the motives of the defense committee. "Under the circumstances, efforts on the part of possibly well-meaning persons to find a racial issue in the case were most unfortunate and created race feelings where none existed."

Young servicemen on their way to combat in the Pacific added to a volatile mix. In the spring of 1943, there were many fights between them and young Mexican American men wearing zoot suits. These suits, popularized by African Americans, Mexican Americans,

The arraignment of the young murder suspects in the Sleepy Lagoon case. Some were found guilty and sent to prison, but the convictions were later overturned.

and Puerto Ricans in the 1930s and 1940s, had high waists, pegged pants, and jackets with oversized shoulders. A wide-brimmed hat and a long keychain completed the outfit.

A Navy base was located about a mile north of the *Times* building, just below the present site of Dodger Stadium. Between the base and downtown was a Mexican American neighborhood known as the Alpine barrio. Sailors walking through the neighborhood on their way to the arcades, girlie shows, bars, and movies downtown often tangled with the tough young men living there.

One night a sailor was injured when he got into a fight in the Alpine barrio with several Mexican American young men. Two days later, about fifty sailors left the base carrying concealed weapons and headed into the barrio, targeting anyone who wore a zoot suit. Hostilities escalated overnight, and servicemen swarmed through downtown, attacking Mexican Americans, whether or not they were wearing zoot suits. For the next four days, civilians joined with servicemen in attacks on Mexican Americans, moving from downtown across the Los Angeles River into the Eastside. Mexican Americans were pulled from movie theaters and stripped of their zoot suits. On June 7, more than five thousand servicemen and civilians roamed downtown, looking for trouble. Taxi drivers offered free rides to whites who wanted to join in. The riot spread south, to predominantly African American Watts. Finally, the military declared Los Angeles off limits to sailors, soldiers, and Marines, bringing the city under control.

THE *TIMES*' STAND

The *Times* condoned the behavior of the servicemen and of the police, who stood aside during the assaults. As the rioting escalated and spread into East Los Angeles, the paper reported, "Those gamin dandies, having learned a great moral lesson from servicemen, mostly sailors, who took over their instruction three days ago, are staying home nights. With the exception of sixty-one youths booked in the county jail on misdemeanor charges, wearers of the garish costume that has become a hallmark of juvenile delinquency are apparently 'unfrocked.'" The reporters got their information from police and sheriffs' commanders. The next day, the paper reported, "in the heaviest street rioting on downtown streets in many years, thousands of servicemen, joined by additional thousands of civilians, last night surged along Main Street and Broadway hunting down zoot suiters." On another day, a page one headline read: "City, Navy Clamp Lid on Zoot Suit Warfare."

The fury of the mob shocked Boyle Heights, especially the Mexican American and Jewish residents. Jews said it reminded them of the pogroms of their native Russia. *La Opinion*, the Latino community newspaper, reported

> various groups of marines and soldiers have attacked Mexican zoot suiters throughout the city of Los Angeles. Although the youth did nothing to provoke the attack, or for that matter resist the attack, many were severely wounded, including women and children. Supposedly the attack has been motivated by past conflicts between the two groups and has been amplified by the press claiming that Mexican youths have been disrespectful toward the servicemen, a claim without any foundation.

Al Waxman, editor of the *Eastside Journal*, a community newspaper with a big Jewish readership, wrote:

> At Twelfth and Central, I came upon a scene that will long live in my memory. Police were swinging clubs and servicemen were fighting with civilians. The officers were making wholesale arrests. Four boys came out of a pool hall. They were wearing . . . zoot suits . . . Police ordered them into arrest cars. One refused. He asked "Why am I being arrested?" The police officer delivered three blows of a nightstick across the boy's head and he went down. As he sprawled he was kicked in the face and police had difficulty loading his body into the vehicle because he was one-legged and wore a wooden limb. Maybe the officer didn't know he was attacking a cripple.

The police tactics provoked strong protests from liberals, including those trying to free the Sleepy Lagoon prisoners. They accused the police and servicemen of racist behavior. Eleanor Roosevelt, wife of the president, articulated their feelings when she wrote in "My Day," her syndicated newspaper column, "The question goes deeper than just [zoot] suits. It is a racial protest. I have been worried for a long time about the Mexican racial situation. It is a problem with roots going a long way back, and we do not always face these problems as we should."

The *Times* disagreed. Its headline over an editorial condemning the president's wife said, "Mrs. Roosevelt Blindly Stirs Race Discord." Her words showed, the editorial said, "an amazing similarity to the Communist party line propaganda, which has been desperately devoted to making a racial issue of the juvenile gang trouble here."

A few days after Mrs. Roosevelt wrote about the case, Philip Murray, president of the C.I.O. industrial union, appealed to President Roosevelt to cool down Los Angeles. He denounced the "rioting and lynch spirit that has been whipped up and directed against citizens of Mexican descent and against

Norman Chandler inspecting the operation of *Times* printing presses. Among his innovations, he acquired a forest products company and newsprint-producing facilities to ensure supplies for the paper's growing needs.

Negroes, most notably in Los Angeles." In response, the *Times* ran an editorial that concluded, "One of the most disturbing aspects of the entire zoot suit affair has been the attempt of certain political and pressure groups to pervert the flare-up into 'racial persecution' or 'race riots.'"

Buff and Norman in his office, looking at the paper's latest edition. OPPOSITE: When Buff Chandler visited, journalists usually paid attention, as is evident in a picture of a working day at the *Times.* Over the years, she tried to improve the appearance of the newsroom. But no matter what changes she ordered, desks soon were piled up again with old newspapers, notebooks, and coffee cups.

BUFF JOINS THE PAPER

In 1944, Norman left on another trip to Europe in search of newsprint, and Buff drove him to the railroad station. She had been asked to be president of the Children's Hospital, where she had been a volunteer. As he prepared to board the train, he told her he hoped she wouldn't accept the hospital presidency. "I need you more than Children's Hospital, " he said. "I want you to come to work for me."

It was quite a transition for someone who had been occupied with volunteer activities, but a welcome one for the restless, ambitious woman. She dug into the opportunity, taking journalism classes at USC. "I took copy reading, headline writing, feature stories," she said. With her husband traveling and her children in boarding schools, she stayed during the week in a small penthouse at the *Times* building. She became his administrative assistant and did a variety of jobs, ranging from supervising building redecorating to helping shape the Times Mirror annual report and her husband's speeches. She took a special interest in the coverage of women and the arts and was responsible for inaugu-

"I was ahead of my time.
I did what I did on my own with no help from anybody."
—Dorothy Buffum Chandler

rating the paper's Women of the Year awards, which were given to more than two hundred women between 1950 and 1976. She paid close attention to the paper and did not like the way L.D. Hotchkiss, the editor, ran it. "I felt it was biased news and I felt the news . . . should not be biased and slanted in any way."

After the war, the civil rights movement that had surfaced in the Sleepy Lagoon case and the Zoot Suit Riot spread through the community. Like Mexican Americans, African Americans became more assertive. A major reason was the return of veterans who came home from war filled with idealism, energy, and fearlessness. They formed new civil rights organizations and invigorated old ones. The G.I. Bill of Rights—one of the great forces of social change in American history—was a tremendous influence, providing college and vocational educations for millions of vets. Many picked California for their postwar homes, often settling in the Los Angeles region, moving into the suburban homes that General Otis and Harry Chandler had envisioned. They had been toughened by the war. A large number were Democrats and many of them liberal. They energized dormant Democratic politics and labor unions. And there was little in the *Times* for them.

Starting the *Mirror*

In 1948, Norman Chandler, impressed by the British tabloids he had seen while traveling, decided to start one in Los Angeles to capture the readership of middle class and working class residents who didn't read the *Times*. The new paper was much more lively than the *Times*. He called it the *Mirror*.

Bill Thomas, who later became editor of the *Times*, started out in Los Angeles on the *Mirror*. He said of the *Times*, "It was a pretty bad paper . . . Nevertheless, it took the news seriously and none of the others did." But he didn't want to work there. He turned down an offer from the *Times* and joined the *Mirror* staff "because it was fun. That's the best time I ever had in newspapers. But it was a loser all the way. We never made any money."

The *Mirror* wanted to connect with Los Angeles's minorities. Managing Editor J. Edward Murray assigned reporter Paul Weeks to do stories on the black community. Some of his colleagues criticized Weeks to his face. "Paul, the way you are writing those stories, you would think you were part nigger," one of them said. The *Times* would not even send reporters into black neighborhoods. Weeks said Murray's decision to investigate Los Angeles's social problems was risky because of the attitude of "his *Times* overseers . . . as I recall the *Times* frowned on the series I wrote for the *Mirror* on the blacks moving into L.A., their problems with employment, housing and education."

OPPOSITE: Norman Chandler (at left) unlocking the door on new building that would house the *Mirror*. A money-loser from the beginning, the paper eventually failed.

Mandate for Change

In 1958, a new editor, Nick Williams, took over. He was an unobtrusive man who had risen from the anonymity of the copy desk to the top job. He was witty in a quiet way and, without flaunting his power, had an air of command about him. He was a different kind of editor, not given to the tantrums or screaming of many of the editors of his generation. Editors and reporters knew he was the boss and felt safe in his hands.

When he was promoted, Williams went to see Norman Chandler and thanked him and said,

> "Now what do you expect me to do?" And he gave me a brief injunction . . . the substance of it was "I want the *Times* to be fair, I want it to be thorough and I want it to tell the people of our circulation what is going on." That's a pretty broad injunction. But in specifics it sounded revolutionary to me because the *Times* had not always insisted on being fair . . . And there was some doubt about it being thorough, and there were considerable doubts about it always telling in its news columns what was going on in Los Angeles . . . So I thought, well boy, if he wants that, I've got a lot of work to do and I'm going to have a lot of fun.

Norman had been changing. He had backed fellow conservative Sen. Robert Taft for president against the more moderate candidate and Buff's choice, General Dwight D. Eisenhower, up until the 1952 Republican National Convention in Chicago. Just before the convention, Norman changed his mind after witnessing an argument between Taft and a news photographer. The photographer was trying to take a picture of Taft and Chandler, who were lunching together. As Chandler and Buff rode back to Chicago from the suburban luncheon, she later remembered, "Norman said that Taft really tore that photographer apart, told him to get away, 'We don't want you around . . . get out of here.' Norman said, 'Senator Taft, I'm a publisher. I'm a newspaper man and I never want to hear anybody talk to a photographer like that, even you.'" He told his wife, "He's lost me . . . now I'm going to vote for Eisenhower." He said Taft showed "how narrow he was."

For much of his career as publisher, Norman Chandler ran the paper much as his father had, supporting Republicans and giving little space to Democrats. Later, he came to believe that the paper should give more balanced coverage and directed his new editor, Nick Williams, to undertake the transformation.

Norman Chandler golfing with Richard M. Nixon.

CREATING NIXON

The most fascinating sign of the change was the *Times*' attitude toward Richard M. Nixon.

The *Times* had created Nixon. One of Norman Chandler's friends, Asa Call, had been a big fundraiser and strategist for the campaign against Upton Sinclair. Call remained a power in Republican and Los Angeles politics for many years after that campaign. One day in the late 1940s, Call's wife returned from a political meeting in Whittier, east of Los Angeles, and told him she had heard a remarkable young candidate, Richard Nixon. Nixon, newly discharged from the Navy, was running against the Democratic congressman, Jerry Voorhis, who happened to have been a Sinclair supporter years before. Call passed word about Nixon on to Chandler and political editor and "kingmaker" Kyle Palmer. The *Times* covered Nixon as if he were a favored son during that campaign and those that followed, through his run for the presidency in 1960.

In 1952, when stories in other papers revealed how Nixon's Southern California business supporters had set up an eighteen-thousand-dollar personal fund for him, the *Times*' editorial said "We Stand By Nixon," who was then the Republican vice-presidential nominee. That year, as David Halberstam related in his book *The Powers That Be*, Palmer suggested to Nixon that he call Norman Chandler and get him to detach the Mirror political editor, James Bassett, to be his campaign press secretary. Two years later, at President Eisenhower's request, Chandler loaned Bassett to the Republican National Committee to help with press relations. In 1956, Bassett was back with Nixon. In 1960, he was dispatched to the Nixon presidential campaign. This time, Halberstam wrote, Bassett was reluctant: "1956 had produced a darker Nixon, there were grim scenes, temper tantrums,

Buff Chandler seems to be enjoying her conversation with Richard Nixon, but later she said she'd found him "sneaky" and had never liked him.

rages against the press, tirades against Ike."

In 1960, with Palmer still in charge of political coverage, *Times* stories about the Democratic National Convention in Los Angeles that nominated John F. Kennedy were as negative and blatantly slanted as anything General Otis might have turned out. That year, a new generation of reporters on other publications and in television news was beginning to cover politics. These journalists dug deeper and were more independent and aggressive than their predecessors. Oblivious to change, the *Times* and its shot-caller, Palmer, continued to protect and celebrate Nixon.

But inside the *Times*, especially at the top, the situation was more complicated. Norman Chandler was troubled by the way the *Times* covered politics. "The *Times* had a reputation of never giving but one side of a labor dispute; we didn't give both sides," he said. "We would give the Republicans all the space they could ever desire. We hardly mentioned the Democratic candidate."

Despite the *Times* endorsement of Nixon, Buff Chandler didn't think much of him. When the fund story came out, Nixon saved his vice-presidential nomination with his famous "Checkers" speech, a maudlin appeal that noted that although the family dog Checkers had been a gift, he was not going to give it back. "I thought it was weak," she said of the speech. "It did not make a favorable impression on me, but I had many other questions about Richard Nixon, anyway, not just 'Checkers.' I knew him very well, for years, since he was first a congressman."

She didn't like him from the day he paid a victorious election night visit to the *Times* newsroom. Norman Chandler asked Nixon, his wife, Pat, his parents, and his brother and sister-in-law upstairs for a snack in a dining room. Nixon, Buff said, "came out in the hall where I was . . . and he said 'Could I have a double bourbon? I don't want my family to see me take it.' So I went in the kitchen and got a double bourbon and he took it in the men's dressing room and he drank it." Disapproval of his sneakiness was "what I feel about Richard Nixon, always," she said. "Watergate and everything else falls into the same pattern."

Norman's doubts about the *Times* political coverage and Buff's skepticism about Nixon would seep down through the paper, influence its approach, and change the nature of California politics.

OTIS IS CHOSEN

In 1960, this shift in the paper's coverage, mild and hesitating under Norman, escalated when Otis Chandler became publisher of the *Times*. The choice of Otis by his parents deepened the rift in the family between Norman's oldest sisters, his two brothers, and Buff Chandler.

According to Buff, the decision was a logical one. She said Norman Chandler was weighed down by the two jobs he was holding, as publisher of the *Times* and president of the Times Mirror Company. Buff said:

> As an observer, I noted that the role of publisher was secondary to my husband. At that time . . . Norman's interest had shifted to the corporate side away from the newspaper side. Whether he knew it or not, I could sense that.

They talked about this when she and Norman were interviewed together. Norman said, "I just couldn't do justice to both jobs." Buff thought that the paper should move more toward the middle of the road, recalling:

> I knew that . . . the only way the *Times* could . . . become a better newspaper, frankly, was to have a publisher that was young . . . It had to be done quickly . . . it's difficult for a man who's been publisher for so many years to give up that precious title. You don't want to have time to think about it . . . do it quickly before you have time to feel sorry about it.

The decision meant that Norman's brother Philip, the *Times* vice-president and general manager, would be passed over for the job of publisher in favor of Otis. The rest of the family blamed Buff. Tad Williamson, son of Norman's sister Ruth, said:

> Buff was a very strong personality and a lot of people felt that she . . . had some psychological problems that were forcing her to do all those things that were . . . offensive. Philip really should have

Philip Chandler, at left, and his brother Norman pose in a crane as work begins on the home of the new *Los Angeles Mirror*. The building was a handsome addition to the *Times* building.

been sort of next in line behind Norm in terms of moving up the ladder at the *Times* . . . And Buff simply wouldn't stand for it . . . I think Buff obviously felt that she had to . . . allow Otis to slip in ahead of Philip . . . I don't know that Philip would necessarily have been the best choice . . . I think he was a very bright fellow, hard of hearing which made things a bit difficult for him . . . he was not a particularly forceful fellow . . . But I think [my] mother's feeling was that he should have had his shot . . . and been able to prove whether he was or was not the best choice.

Otis Chandler said that his mother had told him she had talked to her husband and "had suggested that now might be the time to move Otis up," but the decision, she knew, was up to her husband and the board. "She was not the leader," Otis Chandler said, "My father was the leader . . . my father was very much in control when he was publisher and head of the company. My mother was not running the company."

This point was important to Otis. He made it again with another interviewer.

My mother was a help to my father and contributed to his success . . . He would seek her advice. He would also overrule her all the time when she would come and form an opinion of someone. And he would say . . . for some reason it's gotten turned around that my father was just kind of a caretaker publisher and that she really ran it, and it's not true.

But he also said:

She was always for change and growth and my father, you know, "Things are okay. Why change? Why grow? Why get bigger?"

BUILDING THE MUSIC CENTER

As the 1950s began, Buff's focus was changing. In addition to helping her husband at the paper, she had taken charge of a committee to save the Hollywood Bowl and its orchestra, which had gone broke. That successful fund-raising drive was followed by her most famous effort, raising money to build the Music Center in downtown Los Angeles.

This effort helped move the *Times* away from its exclusively WASP past. Jews had been excluded from a substantial part of Los Angeles life, even though they were a powerful force in the motion picture business, so vital to the area's prosperity and fame. The establishment's clubs, such as the California Club and the Los Angeles Country Club, would not admit them. Downtown law firms would not hire Jews. And old Los Angeles felt the movie industry was vulgar. Jews lived in their own world in Beverly Hills and on the Westside of Los Angeles. There, they built law firms to serve the entertainment business and a country club, Hillcrest, one of the wealthiest. Buff Chandler wanted to break into this wealthy world to raise money.

I decided I would never have meetings in the California Club because they had a very firm policy about no Jewish people as members.

And I'm not like that. Some of my best friends are Jewish. It's what they are that counts with me. I felt the Music Center was going to be something to serve the entire community and not the downtown establishment or the older families of Pasadena and

OPPOSITE: Otis Chandler competes in a weightlifting competition in the 1950s. A shot-putter at Stanford, he maintained a daily weightlifting regimen for most of his life.

here [Hancock Park] . . . To me it did more to break down the barriers against Hollywood, against Jews, against new-timers than anything that's happened in our city.

Time magazine, in a 1964 cover story, called her effort "perhaps the most impressive display of virtuoso money-raising in the history of U.S. womanhood." Her work went far beyond raising money to build and operate the Music Center's three theaters. She enlarged the provincial city's cultural vista. She brought the young composer Zubin Mehta to conduct the Los Angeles Philharmonic. Mehta said when he arrived in Los Angeles,

> Certainly all I heard was that we were in a cultural desert. You don't hear that anymore and it is Mrs. Chandler who we should thank for that. There's no question about it. Without that Music Center, the culture would not have rocketed as it has.

When Mehta was beginning as conductor, he refused to attend symphony board meetings at the California Club. "I said I as an Indian would not be permitted to be a member. I'm not going and she backed me on that." She also supported him when he elevated bass player Henry Lewis, an African American, to be assistant conductor in 1961. "In those days to have a black assistant conductor was not very common," he said. After Lewis chose *Peter and the Wolf* for a young peoples' concert, a City Council member denounced it as Russian propaganda. Mehta said he went to Mrs.

In her pursuit of support for the music center, Buff Chandler persuaded the charming Cary Grant to donate. LEFT: In 1951, after a season of expensive productions failed to attract audiences, the Hollywood Bowl was forced to close. Buff Chandler rescued the cultural landmark by heading up of the Bowl's Emergency Committee and using the *Times* to publicize the Bowl's plight. OPPOSITE: Although her husband and son were the publishers, Buff was a constant presence at the *Times*. Here she is in the mechanical department, watching Otis talk.

Los Angeles Times

★ TUESDAY MORNING, JULY 17, 1951

Rescue Hollywood Bowl!

It was almost as if our sun failed to rise to learn that Hollywood Bowl had suspended its summer season of 1951. But, unlike failure of the solar system, this is something the community can correct.

We cannot afford to let this matter go by the board purely from apathy. The Bowl is our great cultural asset and it gives prestige to this community everywhere. It is a case where we must pay attention "to what the neighbors say."

Committee of Seven

The property is here, the

type of program to be presented caused a lessening of interest in the project.

But the people of this community had not the least idea that Hollywood Bowl was threatened with financial disaster because it was not receiving public support. That lack of public support was the direct cause of suspension. After five performances of "Die Fledermaus" the enterprise was forced to fold.

All hope of a successful season, so we learn now, hinged on the first week's production. Its cost was $67,000, but revenue was only $32,000. Attendance at the five

Chandler and said "I'm new here. I'm just twenty-five years old. What shall I do? She says 'You play it, you understand.' I didn't go the board. I went to her. And Henry did *Peter and the Wolf.*"

Gordon Davidson, artistic director of the Music Center's most inventive theater, the Mark Taper Forum, said:

> one of the functions I think of the theater is to go into areas that are sensitive…to be discussed with people from all different parts of the city and…people of all different colors. I let her know that's what I was going to be doing and she accepted that because she was smart about what that could mean for the Music Center.

Her attitude influenced the paper and became part of the evolution driven by Otis Chandler and carried out by his editors and reporters. Many challenges lay ahead, among them the Watts riots and the other social and cultural upheavals of the 1960s. Progress was slow and often painful, but the paper began to understand long-ignored communities. It had been twenty-two years since the Zoot Suit riot. The old *Times* that had covered that event so poorly was gone. A young and energetic new publisher was in charge.

In her shiny convertible, Buff Chandler seems the picture of idealized Southern California life. But there was much more to her—relentless energy, political skill, and a powerful personality. OPPOSITE: Buff stands in the balcony of the theater that bears her name, the Dorothy Chandler Pavilion, with its elegant chandeliers in the background.

"Otis had a highly progressive editorial policy that cared about the plight of Latinos, cared about the air quality, cared about the massive congestion, and cared about police brutality against the citizens."
—Tom Johnson

"Otis Chandler came of age at a time when journalism was really something that people took very seriously. This is an era in which journalism in terms of the power of news to shape events and to have moral authority was considered to be enormously great." —Alex Jones

"Every parent wants their child to be outstanding. But Otis didn't feel his children were as outstanding as he was. Otis didn't like competition from his children."
—Missy Chandler DeYoung

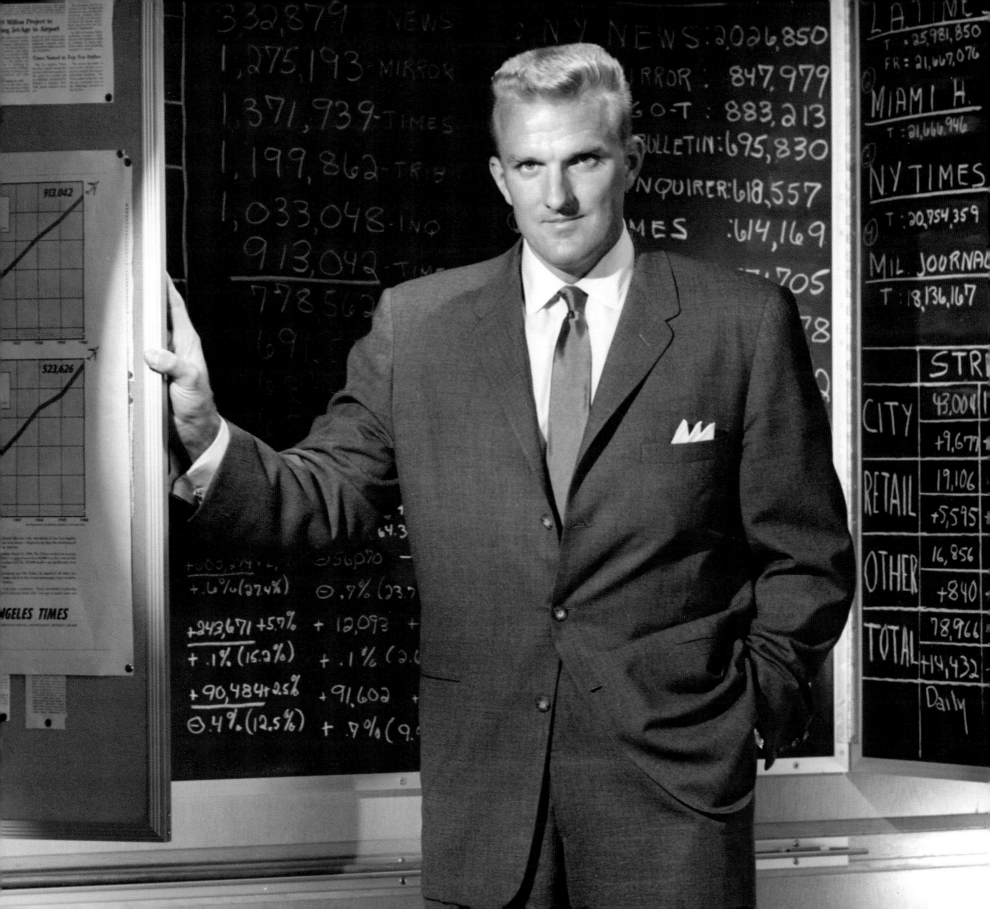

"I WAS GOING TO MAKE SOMETHING OF MYSELF AS AN INDIVIDUAL
APART FROM MAKING SOMETHING OF ME AS A CHANDLER. MY
PARENTS NEVER FORCED ME TO BE THE BEST AT WHATEVER I DO.
THAT SOMEHOW CAME FROM WITHIN ME."

—OTIS CHANDLER

CHAPTER FIVE
Otis Chandler: The Journalist

In 1960, when the young Otis Chandler became publisher of the *Los Angeles Times*, he didn't hang art in his new office. Instead, he had blackboards installed, covering three walls of the large room. He used these boards to record information from the daily reports that reached him from various departments of the paper—the number of pages, the ratio of news to ads, the amount of display and classified advertising, new subscriptions, cancellations, and much more. "Now, of course, it's . . . on the computer, but I did it in chalk," he later recalled. "I wanted to know where I was every day . . . I think I was in the mold of Jimmy Carter. He was a detailist of all detailists as president . . . and that's what I wanted to be. I wanted the people to know all the time what I expected of them."

Otis Chandler's challenge as publisher was to turn a profitable paper scorned by the newspaper industry into a journalis-

The young publisher Otis in his office. PAGES 132-133: In the mid-1950s, Norman and Buff Chandler used the influence of the *Times* to push for legislation to control the smog which shrouded the Los Angeles skyline. PAGES 134-135: Otis Chandler (in white shirt sitting next to second pillar from left) as a reporter in the newsroom. He served a seven-year apprenticeship, working his way through most of the paper's departments. PAGE 136: As part of his preparation, Otis helped out with the printing press. PAGE 137: From left: Otis's sons Harry and Norman raced their father in this 1965 photo.

tic icon that would make more money than ever. He succeeded faster and more triumphantly than anyone—even Otis himself—thought possible.

RADICAL CHANGES

Over the next decade, he hired superior journalists, paid them well, and let them pursue the news, leaving behind the sacred cows, conservative political doctrine, rabid anti-unionism, blind boosterism, and basic lack of curiosity that had long crippled the *Times'* coverage. He greatly expanded the Washington bureau and created a network of bureaus across the nation and around the world. He hired distinguished—or soon-to-be distinguished—journalists to staff them. He enlarged and energized the staff covering Los Angeles and the rest of California with new reporters eager to explore the territory. The *Times* continued to shape Los Angeles, not through biased news stories promoting the publisher's favorite projects, but through the strength of its daily news coverage, investigative reporting, analysis, and editorials. If the old *Times* and the Chandler patriarchs invented Los Angeles, Otis Chandler's paper would be a crucial watchdog as the region reinvented itself—except in one important area:

> The one area I couldn't touch was the [Los Angeles County] Board of Supervisors because they were supporting the Music Center and giving their annual contribution. We weren't able to put our investigative reporters onto the Board of Supervisors even though we had some tips that there were some things that weren't very good. So it's the only area of my publishership that I'm not proud of. I really think I can say that. I think I did about everything else I wanted to do, but I was under constraints. And I deferred to my mother and her interests on that.

That was a significant constraint. The Board of Supervisors was in charge of a variety of services for a county of 9.8 million, from health care for the poor to the biggest potential source of corruption, zoning

Otis visiting the newsroom. He made a point of allowing his editors complete freedom to run this side of the business.

in areas of still-undeveloped land.

The Southland continued to prosper through much of the time Otis was publisher from 1960 to 1980 because of the booming economy and growing population. It didn't need a boost from the *Times*. Otis, himself, declined the behind-the-scenes power role that his grandfather, Harry, enthusiastically embraced and that his father Norman also filled. He was not a member of the downtown establishment, and he let the editors of the paper run the *Times* as they saw fit. He had been asked to head a committee from business, labor, education, and law enforcement. His response:

> I didn't assume that role. I didn't think it was proper for me to assume that role and begin to get back to what my grandfather did, and what Kyle Palmer did, and begin to tell people what to do—the governor and everyone else . . . [My job was being] a catalyst both with the paper by covering news and by having special reports and issues and then by having strong and continuing editorials.

Much of the Southland had been built. The issues were now different. Race relations were a constant challenge. Regulation of coastal development, inconceivable in the wide-open old days, was high on the political and journalistic agenda, as was the preservation of open space in the Santa Monica Mountains and in mountain areas ringing the San Gabriel Valley and in Orange County. The air pollution first tackled by his parents was now the subject of intense and complex regulation. Unlimited residential growth, a virtue in the early Chandler days, was now criticized by homeowners and environmentalists. The Vietnam War, while feeding the Southern California arms industry, was causing increasing casualties and unrest on college campuses.

HALF LION, HALF EAGLE

A former top shot-putter at Stanford and a fanatical bodybuilder, Otis Chandler was an imposing figure. Six-foot three, he had highly developed muscles that were obvious even in a business suit. Among themselves, some of the reporters and editors called him "Shoulders." He inherited the Chandler good looks, although his features were more sharply etched than his father's and his nose longer. With his size and overly developed physique, he resembled a cartoon superhero, an oversized caricature of his handsome forebears.

"Catching a glimpse of Otis Chandler striding through the newsroom was like sighting a griffin; a creature of mythology, half-lion and half-eagle," wrote *Times* columnist Patt Morrison.

He was friendly, straightforward, and approachable. One time, a woman employee, pushing a mail cart, encountered him on a crowded elevator. She looked up and asked, "What's it like being so rich?" Otis thought for a moment and replied, "I don't know. I've never been anything else."

There was a something regal about him, like a benevolent royal in a constitutional monarchy. "After I had been working for Otis for a few years, it occurred to me that I was working for a prince, a man who had been raised to be a prince," said Anthony Day, who was editor of the editorial pages during Otis's regime. He loved being publisher, Day said, "But he also had a prince's sense of entitlement, a sense that perhaps I don't have to do this every damn day."

He had a direct and serious look that told his staff he wanted the straight story, and he had little patience for excuses or bootlicking. He commanded genuine respect, even from the many employees who had little direct contact with him. They respected him for creating a paper where they were proud to work, something new for many of them.

He surfed, hunted game all over the world, biked, raced cars, hiked, and collected expensive vintage cars and exotic motorcycles. In his hunting, surfing, racing, and cycle riding, he courted danger. He enjoyed living on the edge and was somewhat contemptuous of those who weren't risk takers. Even as a boy, recalled his sister Camilla, "something happened to him every summer. He'd get banged up or busted up just doing something."

Above all, he was intensely competitive. "Throughout his life, whether it was the publishing business or hunting or car collecting, [it was] all about competition," said his son, Harry Chandler. " . . . If he couldn't compete well at something, he wouldn't do it. So we all became pretty good skiers, and we never could get Dad to come because he just knew he couldn't keep up with us . . . So rather than competing and losing, he just [said] 'Oh, I really don't like skiing.'"

In 1951, he married another member of the Los Angeles-Pasadena social royalty, Marilyn Brant, called Missy. Her grandfather, Otto Brant, was an officer of Title Insurance and Trust Company and one of Harry Chandler's partners in his real estate

LEFT: Otis lifting weights in 1950. CENTER: The fisherman shows off his catch. RIGHT: Otis shot-putting during his years at Stanford.

ventures. Otis and Missy, traveling in the same circle, had known each other since childhood. They fell in love while attending Stanford and were married in 1951, a match strongly encouraged by Otis's parents. "Otis had a sense of purpose and a sense of dedication when he was in college that few other men had," Missy said. She quickly got pregnant, dropped out of college, and had the first of their five children.

JOINING THE MAJOR LEAGUES

Competitiveness came into play when Otis started attending national publishers' and editors' meetings with his father.

> We weren't being talked about [as] a great paper, even a good paper
> . . . I saw who got the awards, and I saw who served on the boards
> of directors of these newspaper industry groups, and we weren't
> there. I mean, my father, in his day, was elected as an A.P. director
> because . . . [he] was extremely likable, and I think he developed a
> lot of close friends, but he wasn't elected because the newspaper was
> great. He was elected because they liked Norman Chandler. And we
> were excluded from what I would call the "group" of the *New York Times*

Otis and Missy, the new Mr. and Mrs. Chandler on their wedding day in 1951. ABOVE: Otis was an avid outdoorsman. Hunting was, without a doubt, his favorite activity for many years. He displayed many of his hunting trophies in his home and, later, in his auto museum.

Philip Chandler, Norman's younger brother, was executive vice-president of Times Mirror, in line to become the next publisher. But in 1960, Norman passed over Philip to give Otis the top job.

. . . Chicago Tribune, Christian Science Monitor, the Boston Globe, Atlanta Journal and Constitution, sort of the establishment newspapers . . . That really upset me. It was a real wakeup call. You may be a Chandler, and you may be working on the *L.A. Times* but there's no credit in that in terms of your peer group.

He felt part of it was Eastern contempt for the West:

You know, we're out there with the cowboys and Indians and Hollywood and bikinis and all of that. Even though I had gone to Andover. When those people found out I had gone to Andover their faces changed a lot because they assumed I had just gone to Hollywood High or something . . . So I took that away, and I must have said to myself, well, if I ever get the chance, I'm going to make them eat their bloody words.

He understood that much of it was contempt for the *Times* as a newspaper. He started to read the better-regarded papers more closely. "I began to go through page by page and subject by subject and compare, and we weren't very good."

In the mid-1950s Otis believed his uncle and Times Mirror vice-president and general manager Philip Chandler, would be named to succeed his father as publisher. "I just worked hard, kept my nose clean, learned everything I could, made my notes," Otis said. "I took volumes of notes on how everything worked." An example of that was a report he wrote to his father when he was working on the *Mirror* in 1956. For forty-eight pages he relentlessly dissected the operation. By then, the *Mirror* had been successful enough to force the closing of a competing afternoon paper, the *Daily News,* and had taken the title *Mirror News.* But it was still losing money.

Memo on the *Mirror*

"As a perfectionist, I am always critical, perhaps too much, of the departments in which I have worked," he wrote. He went on to say that an assistant managing editor should be replaced "by someone who is a newspaperman." He recommended dumping an assistant city editor who "is not a competent reporter, he cannot even write a simple story, nor can he read copy. He should be fired or put on the police beat as strictly a police beat reporter. If there was ever deadwood in a company, this fat little man is it."

He dug deeply into the details of running the paper, including analyses of photo selection, communications, writing, and precisely how many copies of each edition of the paper were distributed to the staff, compared to how many were handed out, edition by edition, at the *Times*. "I think the *Mirror* draw [distribution] is about twenty percent too high, at least!" he said.

Noteworthy were his negative comments about the *Mirror's* investigative reporting, which was, in fact, excellent and far ahead of its time. The best example of its work was an exposé of a corrupt state official who profited from his power to award liquor licenses. The series resulted in a major reform of state liquor laws and the indictment of the official. Otis was not impressed. He said the city editor "explained that the *Mirror* editorial policy makers believe a newspaper has certain obligations to their readers, and, of these, the most important is their ethical responsibility to expose corruption and tyranny in governmental places.

"They seem to overlook the basic axiom that our company is in business first of all to make money and secondly to print the news." Otis said. "As to which is most important, this ethical responsibility to the reader or the running of a successful business, I have little doubt in my mind . . . here is the *Mirror*, with a deficit operation, and yet still persisting in this business of their ethical responsibility to their readers as a public servant." It was a callow observation, delivered with the know-it-all certainty that comes from being the boss's son. As the years passed, and his chance to take command neared, he changed his mind about investigative reporting, which became one of his paper's great strengths.

On Tuesday morning, April 12, 1960, the *Los Angeles Times* reported on page one that Otis Chandler, at thirty-two, was its new publisher. In an enthusiastic story, top writer Ed Ainsworth described how Norman Chandler made the announcement at a luncheon at the Biltmore Hotel attended by 725 city, state and national leaders. He wrote of "an air of suppressed excitement and expectancy . . . Flashbulbs popped to capture the moment in pictures. A new round of applause spontaneously burst out." In a front-page editorial, Otis Chandler pledged, "No changes are in the offing. A continuation of the successful *Times* format of an unbiased, informed, and responsible press is in order."

This wasn't what he believed. The *Times*, as he saw it, was neither unbiased nor informed. And many changes were in the offing. Making them would require the help of his father, Norman Chandler, for they required big changes in the editorial policy of the *Times* and the very structure of Times Mirror Co.

Otis Chandler New Times Publisher

Follows Father, Norman Chandler, as Fourth Generation to Hold Post

BY ED AINSWORTH

Otis Chandler yesterday was appointed publisher of The Times.

Norman Chandler gave up the position to assume a wider role in the Times-Mirror Co. and allied enterprises.

Announcement of the historic change was made to 725 city, state and national leaders at a luncheon in the Biltmore Bowl.

A member of the fourth generation in direct family descent, Otis Chandler thus assumes charge of The Times in its 79th year. The son of Norman Chandler and Mrs. Chandler, he succeeds his father; his grandfather, Harry Chandler, and his great-grandfather, Gen. Harrison Gray Otis.

In assuming the position of publisher of The Times, Otis Chandler will have charge of the newspaper which for years has printed more news and advertising

Illustrated on Page 3, Part I

disclosure he was about to make.

As a climax, he said:

"I hereby appoint, effective as of this minute, Otis Chandler to the position of publisher of The Los Angeles Times, the fourth in its 79-year history.

"Otis, as my successor, and as my son, I say to you — you are assuming a sacred trust and grave responsibilities. I have the utmost confidence that you will never falter in fulfilling these obligations. This trust is dearer than life itself."

Round of Applause

Flash bulbs popped to capture the moment in pictures.

NORMAN IN A NEW ROLE

Meanwhile, as chairman of Times Mirror, Norman was busy with his own agenda. Backed by a consultant's report and members of the board who were not Chandlers, Norman and Buff wanted Times Mirror to go public and use the capital from stock sales to finance a major expansion and diversification of the company. These changes were opposed by conservative members of the Chandler family, already angered by the decision by Norman and Buff to pass over Philip Chandler in favor of Otis. And in the structure created by Harry Chandler, the whole family controlled the *Times*, although great power was invested in Norman as chairman of the family's Chandler Trust.

In handwritten notes for a family meeting in 1964, Norman Chandler explained the reasons he wanted to put Times Mirror on the stock exchange. Without expansion, the value of stock would drop, the family would lose money and his new team of bright young executives would leave the company. In addition, employee stockholders would be badly hurt. And Times Mirror's "competitors will move ahead & the opportunities will disappear."

He jotted in an informal style: "How wrong it is for a family—not involved—can't know day to day operation & problems & be able to put a noose around our necks & stop progress. They should put faith in management. Other family-controlled

When his father named him publisher, Otis was thirty-two. His response to his father's announcement at the Biltmore Bowl was "Wow!" Before moving on to his prepared remarks, he added that if he were putting the shot, he could do seventy feet and, if trying the high jump, at least eight feet.

businesses I know operate that way," citing Buffum's, the retail business owned by his wife's family. "Lately I have begun to doubt which side [the family is] on," he went on. "[They] should support management or else get out if [they] do not believe in what we are doing."

He wrote, "I feel the risk (infinitesimal) must be assumed by these 4 trustees if the heritage, left by our parents, is to continue to grow and prosper. We cannot stand still. Business is changing. Father would not have wanted a noose around my head . . . have come a long way—now going down the drain."

"What is it," he wondered, "that Buff & I do that makes family appear to resent us?"

Later that year Norman Chandler convinced the other family members to go along. Times Mirror went public and its shares began trading on the New York Stock Exchange. The move financed the purchase of publishing houses specializing in books, maps, bibles, telephone directories, and other newspapers, as well as cable television companies, forests for newsprint material, and newsprint factories. Norman Chandler had made Times Mirror the nation's largest publishing conglomerate.

GOAL OF "MASS AND CLASS"

Years later, Otis said his goal when he took over had been to create "the mass and the class newspaper."

He wanted to increase circulation from its level when he began as publisher, about five hundred thousand daily and nine hundred thousand on Sunday. He said:

> you can't have a million circulation in this market if you just go to the high end . . . the big change and challenge was to keep them and expand . . . to make it a newspaper for the mass reader and that was this huge middle-class, upper-middle, lower-but-not-poor group of wage earners that didn't like the *Times*. They took the *Examiner, Herald Express, Daily News, Mirror.* [The goal is] to push the *Times* into that community by giving them better sports, better news about things that were of concern to them—their jobs, their kids' education, what is happening in lifestyle, culture, news about music, news about sex, news about everything . . . people coverage, people behind the news, Southern California news and then, for the upper group, foreign service, national bureaus, a big Washington bureau, analysis opposite the editorial page with diverse opinions.

In a memo to his top executives, written in 1966, in the midst of the *Times* expansion, Otis accurately forecast the paper's long-range challenge.

> Television is our primary competition both in news and advertising . . . as well as CATV (cable) and the little black box that all the scientists say will be in our living rooms someday bringing us every form of communication at very little cost. Let us reflect upon the thought that the *Times* is not indispensable any more. (I am not sure we ever were.)

Although Chandler did not explicitly anticipate the Internet, the personal computer, or the Blackberry and iPhone, he did understand the challenges that were beginning to face his industry.

He also understood that most of the Chandler family didn't see it the same way:

> The family would have been content—profit increases would have been probably all the family would ever expected. And the Jewish

community and the Black community and the Latino community and the Asian community and all the labor unions would have said, "Well, chip off the old block, he's taken the easy course. The young kid just going right down the center of the road just like his dad did, and that's why we have to have other newspapers in Los Angeles. And . . . the *Times* will be the WASP paper forever."

Otis realized how tricky it would be, trying to expand his audience while holding onto his conservative base:

I didn't want to lose the so-called "class" group of readers—very important opinion molders, very important business leaders, very important academicians. They had to continue to like the *Times* and read it. Also the advertisers. I wanted to make that class . . . still want to take the paper even though they no longer agree with its editorial policy . . . and didn't agree with news about the Jewish community and the black and Mexican community . . . They didn't like seeing a labor dispute covered impartially, all kinds of things they didn't like to see happen to their favorite newspaper because it wasn't that comfortable to read any more. They had to read about the other side of Southern California life and the ethnicity that was changing so rapidly in the Los Angeles market.

Times editor Nick Williams, publisher Otis Chandler, and political analyst Jim Bassett consult in a *Times* conference room. As part of Otis's new regime, the old position of political editor was downgraded to the less powerful job of political analyst. OPPOSITE: Norman Chandler overcame family opposition to have Times Mirror listed on the New York Stock Exchange. Here, Otis and Norman (second and third from left) and Buff (second from right) at the exchange for the listing event. The company's common stock traded at thirty-nine dollars, and Norman bought the first hundred shares.

Otis Chandler is dwarfed by the billboard of a *Los Angeles Times* delivery boy. His goal was to double circulation to a million.

SHIFTING NEWSPAPER SCENE

Together, Norman and Otis Chandler made the decision to kill the *Mirror News*. At the same time—in fact on the same day—Hearst closed the *Examiner*, leaving the morning field exclusively to the *Times*. Hearst merged the *Examiner* with the *Herald*, creating the *Herald-Examiner* with a monopoly in the afternoon. It was a bad decision by Hearst. Metropolitan afternoon newspapers were dying across the country. Traffic was making it too hard to deliver the papers. Americans were watching the nightly news on television instead of reading the afternoon paper. *Herald-Examiner* circulation dropped, particularly after a disastrous strike, while *Times* readership climbed toward a million.

Bill Thomas, *Times* city editor and eventually editor, said that the *Herald-Examiner's* failure to thrive:

> . . . really had a lot to do with making the *Times*. It would have taken a long time to turn that big thing all the way around . . . Otis was just the person to be there . . . You got to hold onto the best of three different newspaper staffs. And obviously dispose of the worst. In other words, you could mold a whole brand new staff, which hardly ever happens to anybody . . . A large part of the making of the *Times* was that we got to do that. It was a totally revitalized and new staff with new ideas. The [old] *Times* was a very stodgy place.
>
> One reason I didn't accept the job in the first place is because you damn near fell asleep there. And everybody was cautious, careful, don't do the wrong thing. It was that kind of a place . . . But all of a sudden here came all these people with totally different ideas. They'd been working for losers. They were not exactly hidebound people. And they were young. And a lot were college graduates—the result of the GI Bill. So we had really a staff . . . that could go after things that hadn't been chased before . . . It became a good paper.

BIRCH SOCIETY SERIES

A 1961 series on the radical right-wing John Birch Society—a huge departure for the *Times*—was an early sign that it might be able to fulfill Otis's hope to create a first-class newspaper. The Birch organization, founded in 1958, had found fertile recruiting ground in the Pasadena-San Marino axis that was part of the *Times'* conservative Republican base. Editor Nick Williams had been receiving mail from Birchers, part of a letter-writing campaign, demanding the impeachment of Chief Justice Earl Warren. As the letter writers became more demanding and abusive, Williams assigned an experienced and careful legal reporter, Gene Blake, to do a series on the Birch Society. Philip Chandler's wife, Alberta, was a member of the society, and Philip Chandler himself was known to be extremely conservative. But Williams also knew that "Norman . . . was not a knee-jerk conservative by any means . . . he had no sympathy whatsoever with, pardon the expression, the kooks of the right."

When Blake's stories were published, Otis asked for an editorial. The first version wasn't tough enough for him, so Williams wrote another one, which Chandler signed and put on page one. In the editorial, he warned that the Birchers' smears were subversive and "will sow distrust and aggravate disputes and they will weaken the very strong case for conservatives . . . " Thousands of Birch supporters cancelled their subscriptions, but many other readers, some of them new, welcomed this declaration of independence and integrity.

Another sign that the *Times* was committed to improving coverage took place in 1962 when it hired the *Examiner's* labor reporter, Harry Bernstein. Bernstein was a liberal and an excellent reporter, who covered both sides of labor-management dispute with fairness and deep knowledge of the issues. In addition, Bernstein saw labor and management conflicts as part of a great social transformation of

Otis spent a good deal of time traveling abroad in the late 1960s as the paper opened new foreign bureaus to expand coverage of world events. RIGHT: A 1961 *Times* series attacking the right-wing John Birch Society offended some, but it also attracted new readers who admired the paper's integrity.

The John Birch Society: What Are Its Purposes?

This is the first of five articles reporting the background, purposes, organization and leadership of the John Birch Society, which has set a national membership goal of 1 million and expects to have 100,000 by the end of 1961.

BY GENE BLAKE

On a wintry day a little over two years ago, a dozen men gathered in Indianapolis at the invitation of a retired Massachusetts candy manufacturer, Robert Welch.

They were influential, busy men. One came from Oregon, one from Kansas, one from Missouri, two from Wisconsin, one from Illinois, one from Indiana, one from Tennessee, one from Virginia and two from Massachusetts.

These men weren't exactly sure why they were there, except that they all shared the same concern over the menace of international communism, its influence in America and the fate of this nation.

Two-Day Explanation

For two full days they listened to Robert Welch set forth his views of the problem and what he thought should be done about it. Out of that meeting of Dec. 8 and 9, 1958, came the John Birch Society.

Within a year there were working chapters in New Hampshire, Massachusetts, Connecticut, New York, Vir-

litical standpoint. In Russia, less than 3% of the 200 million people are Communists and in any country they have taken over there have been no more."

Talbert sees Communist influences working directly here in front organizations, in5trating political organizations and college campuses. But more than that he sees Communist objectives being furthered by certain newspaper writers, in motion pictures, in church pulpits and in all levels of government.

Aims Are Same

"It is sometimes necessary to differentiate between Socialism and Communism, although their aims are the same—leading to the destruction of our constitution and private enterprise," Talbert said.

"There are a lot of things going on in city, county, state and federal government that are certainly driving us into the arms of Socialism. If we continue

conspiracy included former Presidents Roosevelt and Truman, Chief Justice Warren, the late Secretary of-State John Foster Dul-

A REPORT TO THE PUBLIC

Any national organization with a political purpose is of paramount interest to the general public.

Any such organization, methodically yet secretly organizing to influence public opinion, is the public's business.

The John Birch Society is such an organization.

On this page The Times publishes the first of five articles reporting on the founding, the purposes and the operations of the John Birch Society. These articles quote verbatim from the writings of Robert Welch, founder of the John Birch Society, including his manuscript "The Politician," of which photostatic copies are available although it was distributed confidentially to a limited number. The articles also quote extensively from the society's Blue Book, currently used as the society's guide for action, and from leaders of the organization here in Los Angeles.

At the conclusion of this series of articles The Times will publish its editorial opinion of the purposes and activities of the John Birch Society. We suggest in the meantime that each of you, as a free American citizen, read these articles carefully.

NICK B. WILLIAMS
Editor, The Times

Welch, of course, is just one of many who have preached this doctrine of imminent Communist domination to some degree for years. One was the late San Joseph McCarthy who

Southern California and the entire state. When he covered the United Farm Workers union and its charismatic leader, Cesar Chavez, he dealt with economic inequality, farm worker health and safety, and the economic problems facing the agricultural industry, the state, and nation. It was quite a change from the days when Harry Chandler was one of California's biggest owners of farmland, and the paper either slanted or ignored news about labor's early, failed efforts to organize farm workers.

After he lost to Kennedy in 1960, Richard Nixon returned to California for a governorship race he hoped would lead to the presidency. By then Palmer had retired. Otis Chandler hired Carl Greenberg, political editor of the *Los Angeles Examiner*, and Richard Bergholz, who held the same post at the Times' *Mirror-News*. Both papers were now closed because of the deal between Times Mirror and the Hearst Corporation.

The *Times* gave Greenberg and Bergholz the freedom to report the campaign objectively, and they did. They were meticulous reporters, tailing Nixon and his opponent, Democratic Governor Edmund G. Brown, around the state. "We were writing it straight down the middle, and Nixon wasn't used to it. He wasn't aware that the paper had changed, and he was mad when he found out it had," Bergholz recalled years later.

The morning after his loss, Nixon held what he said was his last press conference. After congratulating Brown he criticized the press in a long monologue, beginning with "I want that—for once, gentlemen—I would appreciate it if you would write what I say . . ." and wrapping up many minutes later with, "But as I leave you, I want you to know—just think how much you're going to be missing. You won't have Nixon to kick around any more . . .." In between he praised Greenberg, to the reporter's embarrassment. But he did so only to get back at Bergholz, whom—for reasons known only to Nixon—he blamed for the *Times* coverage.

It wasn't Nixon's last press conference. But for the *Times*, it was a highly significant moment. It was public acknowledgment of what had been clear during the campaign. The paper was no longer a Republican rag. Its reporters could cover their city, state, nation—and the world—in a fair and honest way.

OTIS RECRUITS THE BEST

Otis helped recruit some of the *Times'* newcomers. "I remember Nick Williams said, 'You'll never get him, you'll never get him' and I'd say 'Bullshit, c'mon Nick, we're the *Times*....it was a sales job." Otis said he felt he impressed the recruits with his "maturity, sincerity, ambition, (and) the *Times* looked good; it was going to be the paper of the future."

In the early years of his tenure as publisher, Otis noticed the work of Paul Conrad, the liberal *Denver Post* cartoonist. Conrad remembered receiving a call from Nick Williams. The editor said the paper's cartoonist had died, and they were looking for a

OPPOSITE: Otis Chandler appears with Robert Kennedy in July 1964 at the Los Angeles Coliseum. Although it was a sporting event—a U.S.-Russian track meet—Bobby was then seeking the U.S. vice-presidency.

"THE KENNEDYS SEEM TO GET ALONG OKAY AND THE ROCKEFELLERS SEEM TO GET ALONG OKAY. BUT THE CHANDLERS, BOY. IT'S REALITY AND WE HAVE TO DEAL WITH IT."
—OTIS CHANDLER

replacement. Conrad recalled that Williams told him "Otis said the only one I want is Conrad." Conrad didn't believe the call was authentic. So he hung up, found the phone number of the *Times* in a newspaper directory and called Williams back, confirming that it was, indeed, the editor himself. Williams picked up Conrad at the airport and took him to meet with Otis at a club. Otis said, "Come down tomorrow, take a look at the paper, read some editorials that we've been working on and some we've printed, and see what you think."

"It was marvelous, marvelous stuff," Conrad said. "So, I said 'Well, sounds good enough for me. The price is right, so I'll be here. Came back, got off the plane and I told [my wife] Kay, 'We're moving to L.A.'"

Conrad's devastating cartoons skewering Republican idols Nixon and Reagan infuriated conservative *Times* readers, including Ronald Reagan and his wife Nancy, but attracted many new ones. Jim Murray, Otis's new sports columnist, who soon became the nation's best, drew many more readers to the paper.

Despite early signs of improvement, change was slow at first. Paul Weeks noted this in 1962 when the *Mirror News* folded, and he moved over to the *Times*. City editor Bill Thomas assigned him to cover race relations in Los Angeles. Weeks said blacks were "at first suspicious of anyone wanting to put anything in the white press about them. And I didn't blame them." He recalled reporters covering the police "characterizing murders, rapes, and so on among blacks as misdemeanor crimes," not worthy of coverage. "When the crime became black upon white," Weeks went on, "it could reach headlines."

Weeks said his bosses turned against him when he protested the ejection of a black reporter working for the *Sentinel*, an African American newspaper, from a meeting of a segregationist organization in 1964. They said Weeks refused to cover the meeting. Whatever the reason, Weeks was taken off the civil rights beat. At the time, he told his editors, "This town is going to blow up one of these days and the *Times* won't know what hit it."

It was a real coup for the paper when Otis Chandler (right) persuaded Paul Conrad, political cartoonist for the *Denver Post*, to join the *Times*. Conrad went on to win three Pulitzer Prizes. OPPOSITE: Race-car driving was one of Otis Chandler's great passions. Here the Chandlers gather around Otis's Porsche: from left to right: son Harry Chandler, Otis's wife Missy, son Michael, daughters Carolyn and Cathleen, son Norman and daughter-in-law Jane. Otis, at the wheel of the car, holds his grandchild and namesake, Otis Yeager Chandler.

WATTS RIOTS

His prediction proved accurate the following year, with the Watts riots. This event was a turning point for Otis and the *Times*.

Otis was prepared. He had now been publisher for five years. He had broken out of the *Times* cocoon and made it a point to travel around the community. After giving speeches, he said

> I would start working the room. I didn't drink, and after a short while I was enjoying myself fully. I would meet interesting people, and I would develop this circle of friends. I wanted to meet Democrats and Republicans and Independents and Latinos and Blacks, and Jewish, Asian—there wasn't any group I didn't feel was important to me and to the *Times*. So I went out a great deal.

> I tried to strike a balance between those that are important in the community as leaders and those that live in the community who are primarily not important but they're either private individuals or small business owners or they have a church in Watts. So through my years, I went into minority communities and visited them on their home turf—I had no fear for myself. I had no racial prejudice. I had no feelings of "this is heroics" . . . I felt it was very important to do.

At the time of the riots, Bill Thomas, who had been city editor of the *Mirror News*, was running the *Times* city desk, and it was a far different operation than in the past.

Thomas dispatched his white reporters into south central Los Angeles, dangerous territory for them. Editors recruited a young African American man from the advertising department to help with reporting. Thomas had a staff that, as he put it:

> . . . could do the things you had in mind . . . I remember running up and down the aisles with story ideas and talking it over with people. And they said for Sunday? And I'd say tomorrow. And so we'd put about forty stories in the paper in one day. Let's do it today, it's not going to get any better by Sunday. And you can do it if you try. And so we did it. We did a lot of things.

On August 11, 1965, the Watts riots were set off by an altercation between a white California Highway Patrol officer and Marquette Fry, an African American man. The violence took the city by surprise, but the *Times* tackled the story and won a Pulitzer Prize. Almost a year later, Watts exploded again in a smaller riot, as did Hunters Point in San Francisco.

After the Watts riots, Thomas met with angry African American leaders. "I'd meet them in a bar, and we'd talk." He also had meetings with them at the paper, and Otis sat in. Otis had his own meetings, and noted:

> They just disliked the police all the way up to the police chief . . . I didn't have any professional training in defusing racial relations, but there was no one else and they did trust me . . . I would say, "OK, I hear what you're saying, and I will . . . talk to the police chief and see if there's something that can be done."

Thomas dispatched reporters throughout the community to find out what had caused the riots. The resulting stories won the Pulitzer Prize but failed to make a permanent impact on South Los Angeles and its problems. The area's economy worsened. The few remaining factories closed. Businesses fled the area. The schools got worse. Although *Times* reporters occasionally wrote about South Central, their stories couldn't stop the decline.

TRANSFORMATION COMPLETE

An excellent way to see the changes Otis brought to the paper is to look at its front page.

On the day he took over in 1960, the dreary page was filled with wire-service stories from Italy and South Africa, one on an aborted rebellion against Fidel Castro and a short wire dispatch on President Eisenhower's departure for a golfing vacation in Georgia. The four-paragraph Ike story was so routine and uninformative that it scarcely merited a place in the paper, much less on page one. But when Marilyn Monroe committed suicide in 1962 there were two bylines on the stories, and there was another on a piece headlined, "Sad Child, Unhappy Start." Bylines had become important in modern newspapers. They gave life and per-

In 1970, while many other papers still supported the Vietnam War, the *Times* wrote an editorial advocating the U.S. pull out of the conflict. Under Otis's leadership, the paper greatly improved coverage of science, particularly aerospace, to meet the challenges of the space age and new discoveries.

Although Otis preferred a quiet life, he felt obligated as publisher to spend time making public appearances. At left, he sits next to Barbara Walters at a banquet. CENTER: a formal portrait of Otis. RIGHT: Otis greeting visitors touring the *Times* Building.

sonality to a newspaper and let readers know that an actual person had written the story, giving them someone to blame or praise. Bylines also helped break up the gray appearance of the newspaper pages.

On May 18, 1980, as Otis Chandler's regime was ending, the stories on the front page were a powerful illustration of what he had accomplished. Jeff Prugh reported from Miami on fifteen dead in racial rioting. Staff reporter Gaylord Shaw was at Mount St. Helens, where six had been killed by the volcano's eruption. *Times* reporter Tyler Marshall wrote from Pakistan, and David Lamb from Africa. Joan Sweeney reported on efforts to mold evangelical Christians into a political movement, a piece far ahead of its time. John Goldman in the New York bureau described the problems songwriters were having selling their music. Finally, Austin Scott—an African American reporter who would not have been hired before Otis took over—wrote a story that never would have made it into the pre-Otis *Times*: "Poor Squeezed Hardest by Housing Shortage in L.A."

Struggles with Local News

Yet, with all these accomplishments, Chandler and his paper struggled to find the best way to cover the vast metropolitan area it served.

For one thing, the size and sprawling nature of the metropolitan area were daunting. Los Angeles was the biggest city, but it was one of many. Places that had been towns in the Harry Chandler and even Norman Chandler days were incorporated cities, with their own governments and problems. The circulation spread over five counties—Los Angeles, Orange, Ventura, San Bernardino, and Riverside—encompassing urban, suburban, and even rural life.

The solution was to publish zone editions, each with its own editors and reporters. Most came out twice a week, although the Orange County and San Fernando Valley editions were daily. From their offices, the reporters—most of them young—covered

Otis Chandler reveled in the outdoor life. **LEFT:** It's a tight fit for the muscular Otis and the baby in this small wading pool. **CENTER:** Otis showing off his muscles at Lake Powell in Arizona. **RIGHT:** The Chandlers were a family of surfers, a sport they often enjoyed at Dana Point.

great stories, such as the transformation of the San Gabriel Valley from white to Asian and Latino. The story of that valley, in fact, was the story of L.A. But because most of the articles only appeared in the San Gabriel Valley edition, the rest of the Southland was unaware of a demographic revolution that would impact their lives. With this system, the paper's readers got a fragmented picture of the area's problems with air pollution, crime, transportation, and employment, all of which had to be dealt with on a regional basis. And some of the zone editions didn't have enough reporters—or newspaper space—to adequately cover the cities and school districts in their areas. Eventually, these local sections were discontinued because of cost.

PRESSURE ON OTIS

During these years, Otis felt under constant pressure, as he explained:

> . . . pressure because I had to produce. I'm sure certain members of the family . . . didn't like my editorial policy and the changes in the *Times*. I'm sure they were hoping I would fail. And they were hoping for the paper to have someone put in by the board of directors that would take the paper back to the paper that their parents liked, that they grew up with, that their friends liked . . .

He was right. The conservative Chandlers criticized the changed paper. Their complaints touched off a family fight at a meeting of the board of the Chandis Securities Co., one of the entities created by Harry Chandler to assure continued family control and shield his descendents from taxes. Philip Chandler complained that the paper had veered from the policies of General Otis. The paper had become middle-of-the-road, even liberal. Defending Otis, May Goodan, another of Harry Chandler's children, told her siblings that their father had not, in fact, followed General Otis's policies or style of journalism. Reading habits change, she said, requiring a different kind of journalism. Perhaps so, said another brother, Harrison Chandler, but basic conservative beliefs don't change. Norman, trying to make peace, said he didn't think there had been any change in basic *Times* editorial policies. It was still a conservative Republican paper, he said, and he assured his family that he supervised the editorial policies and

was responsible for them. It was clear from the dispute that only Norman Chandler and May Goodan—especially Norman—stood between the conservative Chandlers and the young publisher remaking the paper.

What was striking about this period, which employees came to view as a golden age for the *Times*, was that none of the reporters and only a very few of the editors had any idea their publisher was under such intense pressure. One of Otis's policies was to shield the editorial department from interference by the paper's advertising department and business affairs. This ensured the paper's journalistic integrity. Besides, most writers and editors were uninterested in such matters. They thought their world was secure and Otis Chandler invincible.

Norman Chandler (standing at rear behind chair), presiding over a meeting of Times Mirror executives and family members, including Otis (standing far right) and Dorothy (sitting far right). His vote carried more weight than those of the other board members. OPPOSITE: Otis working at his desk in the publisher's office.

HUMILIATION OF GEOTEK SCANDAL

That perception ended on August 11, 1972, when they read in the *Wall Street Journal* that Otis had fallen victim to two old Los Angeles ailments: greed and the temptation to speculate in oil. The idea of underground wealth waiting to be tapped had an irresistible appeal in Los Angeles. C.C. Julian had understood this when he sold shares in his oil company to the wealthy back in the 1920s. A half-century later, a new C.C Julian arrived. His name was Jack Burke, and he was Otis Chandler's dear friend from the days when they were on the Stanford track team. Burke had started an oil exploration company, GeoTek.

Chandler's first wife, Missy, recalled:

Jack was our perennial houseguest for fifteen years . . . he told jokes that had me howling and crying, and he told them so well. He kept Otis laughing. Otis and I were not wealthy. Otis was always trying to find schemes to make money . . . We had a big house and five kids, and he would take a lot of that and spend it on his hunting trips. So Jack said, "I'm going to help you make money. You become part of my company, and I'll put you in with these oil leases if you'll bring in some investors." And Otis did. So he called all his friends and my friends and said, "Look, this is a good deal. It's a good tax write-off" . . . Otis trusted his friend Jack . . . I had a couple of run-ins with Jack and asked him to leave the house . . . but Otis would always invite him back. So what do you do with a friend like that? . . . Turns out Jack was a criminal and we didn't know it.

Among those Otis contacted on behalf of GeoTek were relatives, as well as Art Linkletter, Kirk Douglas, Nancy Sinatra, Jack Kent Cooke (then owner of the Los Angeles Lakers), and Evelle J. Younger, district attorney of Los Angeles County. Otis

A rare reunion of the Chandler clan in 1984. Bitter dissent between family members kept them at odds.

himself invested more than two hundred thousand dollars. But he didn't disclose to the other investors what he was receiving from Burke finder's fees and promotional shares, which totaled almost five hundred thousand dollars. More than thirty million dollars were invested in GeoTek over eight years. The Securities and Exchange Commission charged that Burke had siphoned off the oil investment money for his own personal use.

When the *Wall Street Journal* broke the story, Otis was humiliated. The headline read, "Wealthy Acquaintances of California Publisher Evidently Lost Bundle; Otis Chandler 'Opened Doors' for College Pal Who Ran Oil Fund, SEC Now Probes." The case dragged on for several years before a federal court sentenced Burke to thirty months in prison. But the SEC dropped charges against Otis, although he had to pay more than a million dollars in legal fees. "Otis was so embarrassed when the story came out in the *Wall Street Journal* that he didn't want to go anywhere and didn't want to do anything," said Missy. "I said, 'Look, Otis, you're not guilty . . . you're going out there, and you're going to hold your head up high . . . '"

His son Harry said, "Some of the investors were relatives and friends from Pasadena who suddenly were looking at our family like they've been led down a path . . . they had lost some or all of their investments. So it was a tough few years." Otis Chandler had to apologize to family and friends. It was an embarrassing time and a mistake his enemies in the family would hold against him.

Otis near the end of his years as publisher. Constant pressure from the family was beginning to wear him down. RIGHT: A *Wall Street Journal* story describing how Otis Chandler enticed family, friends, public officials, and celebrities into questionable investments with GeoTek, a company owned by an old friend.

VOL. CLXXX NO. 29 ★ ★

Price of Friendship

How Rich Acquaintances Of California Publisher Evidently Lost Bundle

Otis Chandler 'Opened Doors' For College Pal Who Ran Oil Fund SEC Now Probes

$30 Million Down the Hole?

By HERBERT G. LAWSON
Staff Reporter of THE WALL STREET JOURNAL

SAN FRANCISCO—Otis Chandler, scion of a famous and powerful publishing family, distinguished himself at Stanford (class of '50) by setting a Pacific Coast Conference shotput record.

One of his best friends as an undergraduate was another track man, Jack P. Burke, a discus thrower who didn't set records and seemed to bask in the reflected glory of Mr. Chandler. When the yearbook came out, somehow, Mr. Burke's senior picture was omitted. "He was an also-ran," sums up one Stanford man.

After college, Mr. Chandler's ascendancy in the newspaper world was assured, and in 1960 he became publisher of The Los Angeles Times, the paper his family controls. Mr. Burke became a stockbroker and then a San Francisco-based promoter of oil-drilling ventures after a successful wildcat investment. The Chandlers and the Burkes (their wives became chums) found much in common, and Mr. Burke became godfather to Otis Chandler's first daughter, Cathleen. The two men, sharing a love of physical challenge, traveled to Africa, Alaska and, recently, to Mongolia or hunting expeditions.

But the camaraderie is gone now, destroyed by a bizarre and until now unpublicized financial disaster in the go-go world of oil-drilling funds. In the shambles of that friendship is perhaps the most embarrassing mishap ever to befall the 44-year-old publisher.

An Intense Investigation

Mr. Burke promoted and operated oil-drilling partnerships with considerable help from Mr. Chandler. A wide circle of the publisher's friends, including many top executives at the Times, leading political and society figures in

NORMAN'S PASSING

On October 20, 1973, Norman Chandler died at his home of throat cancer after a long, painful illness. Otis's great source of strength in the Chandler family war was gone. As Norman was dying, Nixon promised to come by and see him. "Norman was by then quite weak," said Peter Fernald, a retired Times Mirror executive. "And knowing that Richard Nixon was coming, he got all dressed up—coat, tie and everything . . . And Nixon never showed up and never phoned in his regrets. They just waited and nobody ever appeared."

Norman's death was not only the loss of a beloved husband for Buff Chandler, but also the end of her days at the *Los Angeles Times*. On May 9, 1975, less than a half a year after Norman's death, she met with Otis, Times Mirror president Robert Erburu, and Dr. Franklin Murphy, chairman of the Times Mirror executive board. The purpose of the meeting was to tell Buff her job at Times Mirror had been eliminated. Franklin Murphy, whom Buff had helped lure to the *Times* when he was chancellor of UCLA, followed up the meeting with a cold letter setting down the terms of her dismissal. The terms: off the payroll by May 19, 1976; out of her corporate office in the plush Atrium immediately and into a less prestigious space elsewhere in the building. She was allowed to use her new office until she left the company. Now that Norman was gone, there was no one to take her side or protect her.

Another family matter occupied Otis. At the height of his power as publisher, he found himself unhappy in his marriage. He fell in love with Bettina Whitaker, who worked in public relations. "I was a happy person in my career and a happy person with my friends and family, but I was an unhappy husband," he said. He and Missy had been married twenty-seven years.

The GeoTek scandal deeply humiliated Otis. Although charges against him were dropped, the episode ended up costing him a million dollars in legal fees. OPPOSITE: Norman Chandler in old age—the quintessential Southern Californian. He loved the sunshine, his swimming pool, and his copy of the *Los Angeles Times*.

"I was the last one to know that he had a mistress," Missy said. She had gone back to school and was engaged in many volunteer activities, including the Otis Art Institute, named for the family founder. "And I was getting more like Buff. Or so Otis said: 'Don't be like Buff. I don't want you to be like my mother.'" Missy received a master's degree in urban planning from UCLA, worked for the Howard Hughes organization in planning its properties, and then opened her own firm. "I don't think Otis liked that," she said. "He thought I was competing with him. I really wasn't. I was competing with other architecture planning firms."

Otis had met Bettina in 1978 through his race-car driving. They'd had a brief encounter at a planning session for an event in which Otis was to compete, a six-hour endurance race at Watkins Glen, the New York auto-racing complex. Bettina was at the meeting, and later at the race, representing Shakey's, one of Otis's sponsors. On the day of the race, Otis recalled:

> Bettina flew in and . . . I recognized her coming down the aisleway at the airport . . . So I went up and gave her a little peck on the cheek . . . I couldn't figure out why I did that 'cause I hadn't really ever talked to her you know, just that one meeting in my office.

She joined Otis, his sons and the rest of the team for meals. They all stayed at the same motel. That event marked the beginning of a deepening friendship between Otis and Bettina.

Shakey's wanted her to move from Pasadena to Dallas. She preferred California. Otis put her to work at the *Times* in circulation marketing. While on a trip to the family home in Montana with Missy and their daughter Carolyn, he went to a pay phone and called Bettina. "I started to cry," Otis said, and he told Bettina, "'I really love you and want you to marry me' . . . She said 'yes.'" Otis returned to the cabin. He first told Missy and then Carolyn about Bettina. His daughter was furious. "Daddy," she said. "How could you! You're so mean!"

The crisis escalated when Missy swallowed a vial of sleeping pills:

> I dumped her in the car, took her to the nearest clinic and made it in about two minutes to have her stomach pumped or she would've died. And I felt horrible, of course, about Missy almost dying, but I didn't feel horrible about what I'd done 'cause I did it very nicely. I didn't scream at her, I didn't yell . . .

Otis and Bettina married in 1981.

In the next few years, Times Mirror continued to prosper. New enterprises were added. Monopoly status permitted the *Times* to raise advertising rates every year. Years when income stalled or slightly dropped were handled without cutbacks or staff cuts. Otis Chandler continued as publisher until 1980, when he took his father's old job as chairman of Times Mirror Co. The company made big profits as the Southern California economy grew and even managed its way through the decline of the aerospace industry after the Vietnam War and the loss of big tire and auto manufacturing plants.

Bill Thomas, editor since 1971, put his own distinctive stamp on the paper. Earlier in his career, he'd loved working as city editor of the *Mirror*, with its old-fashioned diet of several editions a day, each featuring a new story or a new angle, with short, punchy stories. But as editor of the *Times*, he looked for something more. He sought reporters who could burrow into the depths of a story, digging out facts, subtleties, motivation, telling it as a novelist might. This involved closely observing the people involved, their physical appearance, habits, foibles, manner of speech, dress, relations with others, the myriad of details that reveal us as individuals. Sometimes the reporter would dig deep into injustice, find the cause, the villain, the victim and, if one existed, the hero. All this took time and patience. A reporter might have to hang out with someone for weeks or months. Documents had to be found and explained. Unwilling men and women had to be cajoled into granting interviews and answering questions. Finally, the reporter had to sift through the material, organize it and write it into a compelling story. This form of writing, known as literary journalism, attracted writers who felt bored and restricted by the brief recitation of facts demanded by most newspapers. Some of the best of them came to the *Times*.

Otis worried the stories were too long, but Thomas persevered. "I couldn't imagine a better publisher," Thomas said. "He put his money where his mouth was. He said he wanted a good newspaper, and he hired people and then he let them make a good newspaper. He didn't try to micromanage . . . if a job being turned in was not what he was looking for, he'd get rid of you. But as long as you had the job, you did the job. He didn't care to talk an awful lot about how you were doing the job, just what the result was."

On April 14, 1980, at the annual *Times* editorial award dinner, Otis had a surprise for the big editorial staff that filled the ballroom. Instead of giving his usual "state of the paper" speech, he presented his successor, Tom Johnson, a Lyndon Johnson protégé whom Otis had met when buying LBJ's family television station in Austin, Texas. By the time Johnson was introduced, some attendees had lost interest in the awards and were barely listening to the program. But Otis's words caught everyone's attention. The announcement of Otis's retirement came as a shock. It was not good news.

LEFT: Otis Chandler speaking at the Times Editorial Awards banquet in 1980. His announcement that he was retiring came as a surprise to most in the audience. CENTER: Tom Johnson, the new publisher, walking up to take his place at the podium. RIGHT: Johnson addressing the gathered editorial staff for the first time as publisher.

By 1989, the *Los Angeles Times* was considered by many in the industry as one of the country's three great metropolitan newspapers, along with the *New York Times* and the *Washington Post*.

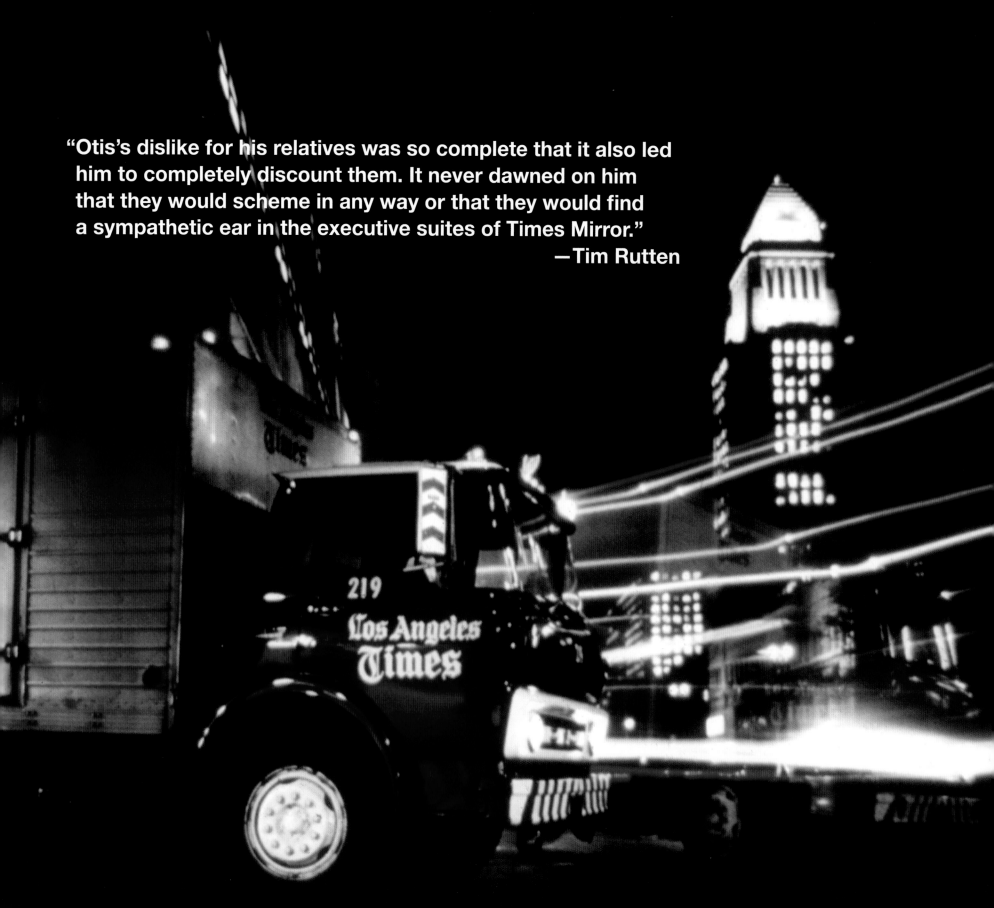

"Otis's dislike for his relatives was so complete that it also led him to completely discount them. It never dawned on him that they would scheme in any way or that they would find a sympathetic ear in the executive suites of Times Mirror."
—Tim Rutten

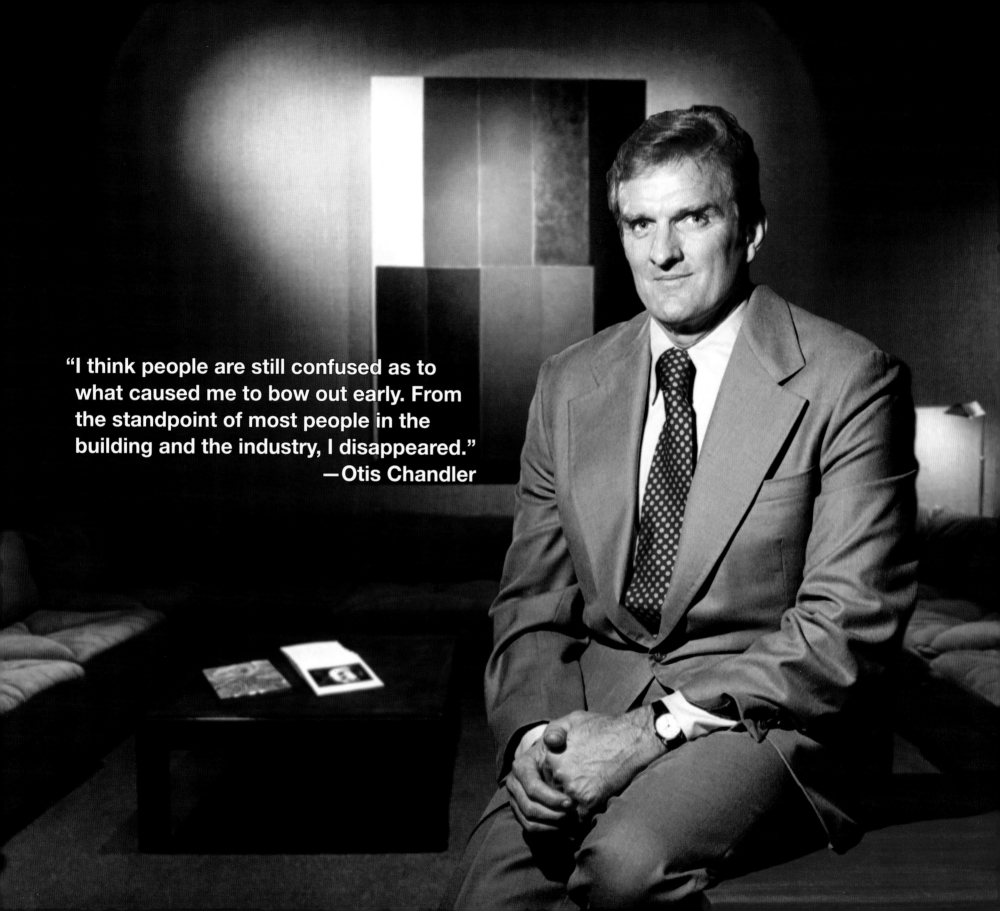

"I think people are still confused as to what caused me to bow out early. From the standpoint of most people in the building and the industry, I disappeared."
—Otis Chandler

IN EVERY RESPECT BUT BLOOD, THE CHANDLER DYNASTY CONTINUED UNDER TOM JOHNSON, THE MAN OTIS TREATED LIKE THE BROTHER HE NEVER HAD.

CHAPTER SIX

Tom Johnson: The Successor

Otis Chandler and Tom Johnson were partners in the final years of the *Los Angeles Times*' dominance in the Southland. The two, who became as close as brothers, would eventually see their great hopes for the paper shattered. But their friendship, strained at times, outlasted their careers. Years later, Otis would write Johnson:

You have always seemed like an older son to me, or that younger brother I never had. I feel so blessed and fortunate to have crossed your path in Austin . . . I was tremendously impressed from the beginning with your obvious leadership qualities.

Tom Johnson was the first *Los Angeles Times* publisher who was not a member of the Chandler family. He was born in Macon, Georgia, and went to work as a reporter at the *Macon Telegraph News* at the age of fourteen. He said he

found it to be interesting work and became addicted to it very early and never really thought about doing anything else. I discovered

Tom Johnson became publisher in 1980, and Otis Chandler moved into his new post as editor-in-chief of Times Mirror and then the company's chairman. PAGES 168-169: The Los Angeles Times building is part of an undistinguished cityscape predating downtown's high-rise office buildings. This is the view from City Hall. PAGE 170: When the printing presses were still in the building, *Times* delivery trucks, loaded with the latest edition, rumbled out of the building from early evening until the next morning. PAGE 171: A view of the *Times* corporate offices through the atrium on the top floor. PAGE 172: Otis Chandler in his executive office. PAGE 173: Otis polishing an antique Rolls-Royce in his vintage car museum in Oxnard, California.

my professional passion—journalism—in Macon. I developed this overwhelming desire to excel; maybe it was something about growing up on the wrong side of the tracks. I think I first become aware of my identity when I saw my very first byline in the Macon paper. That was the editor saying this story was good enough to put [my] name on it. I said, "Gee, I've done something that was worthy of a byline."

The paper's publisher, Peyton Anderson, was so impressed by the young Johnson that he helped send him to the University of Georgia and then to Harvard, where he received an MBA. He became a White House fellow, working in the press office under Bill Moyers and, later, George Christian. Tom Johnson had promised to return to Georgia to help Anderson run the paper. But President Lyndon Johnson (no relation) wrote Anderson, saying he would like the young man to remain in the White House:

Tom feels a strong moral commitment to return to Macon because of everything you have done for him. His conscience won't let him just walk away from that commitment . . . He is torn between knowing that I need him and his desire to honor your confidence. I wanted you to know this, and also to say that if you can spare Tom Johnson, his country and his President need him.

Anderson gave his permission, telling the president, "He can live up to any expectancy you may have of him. It is now your responsibility to see that he get that chance." And then, reminding Johnson that one good turn deserves another, Anderson wrote a P.S. asking the president to appoint a local lawyer as a judge.

All of President Johnson's family became close to Tom. A friend described him as "advisor to the president and the advisor to the nervous bridegrooms of the White House brides."

He was a tall sandy-haired man, intelligent, sensitive, and considerate of those around him. He wielded his power with his intellect, his ability to project a vision for the future, and loyalty to his subordinates, which was repaid in kind. On the night of the *Times'* awards banquet, when Otis Chandler introduced Johnson as publisher, he was bright and youthful looking at thirty-nine, still with a trace of the eager young staff member known as "boy wonder" at the White House. The term was used with the sort of affection Luci Johnson expressed in a note to him on his fortieth birthday: "You may no longer be a boy, but you'll always be a wonder."

When he left the White House, President Johnson brought Tom back to Texas with him to head the family-run television station in Austin. There Otis Chandler met Johnson in 1972 after Times Mirror bought the station. Chandler, Al Casey, president of Times Mirror who had led the company's diversification program, and Robert Erburu, an executive who would eventually succeed Casey, flew to Texas to look over the new property. Casey had completed the sale after weeks of arduous negotiations with the former president, and the Californians were meeting about three hundred Texas dignitaries at a reception. Tom Johnson remembered all the dignitaries' names, including those of the spouses. Otis told him, "I've never seen anybody who was able to remember every single name, not only of the individual and his or her [spouse] but also a little something about them."

When Johnson arrived in Los Angeles, the paper and the Southland were booming, and Times Mirror seemed as solidly rooted in Southern California as the area's other corporate giants, such as ARCO, Union Oil, Security Pacific Bank, and several big department store chains—all of them since gone. In 1980, having grown from the seeds planted by Harry Chandler, the area's economy was in a period of remarkable expansion in the city as well as north to Ventura County and east into once-rural Riverside and San Bernardino counties. Topping it all was the population and economic explosion in Orange County, where Otis Chandler had built a large satellite printing plant and started the Orange County edition. A similar plant was built in the San Fernando Valley and an edition started there.

Chasing "mass and class"—the Otis Chandler formula—the paper followed the population. Circulation exceeded a million. And, as the largest paper with the greatest reach, the *Times* had a virtual advertising monopoly. From the time Johnson became president of the *Times* under Chandler in 1977 and then through his reign as publisher, the paper opened six new foreign bureaus and five domestic ones. Spending on news gathering grew by more than three hundred percent. By the end of the decade, profits were up almost thirty percent. Los Angeles was full of promise. Its business leaders, and the *Times*, saw the area as the

Otis Chandler meeting President Lyndon Johnson in the White House in the mid-1960s. The paper's next publisher, Tom Johnson, had close ties to LBJ and his family.

gateway to Asia, a leader in what was grandiloquently called the Pacific Rim.

The *Times* was also at its journalistic height. Talented reporters and editors had been recruited to staff a large Washington bureau, as well as domestic and foreign bureaus. Along with state and local reporters, the large staff provided a rich variety of daily news. The paper continued to be criticized for being more interested in Asia than Los Angeles, and local reporters had to fight hard for attention and space. Still, as a package, the paper tried to provide something for everybody.

As the decade of the 1980s continued, the city began to experience new problems. Unemployment rose in some areas; retail sales started to stagnate; homelessness increased. Los Angeles and even some of the surrounding areas were losing the home-owning middle class that had been the economic base of the paper and much of the Southland. The end of the Cold War idled aerospace and other industries. Supermarkets and department stores—old brands like I. Magnin, The Broadway, Bullock's, May Company, and Robinson's—all were eventually swallowed up by Federated, parent company of what would be a single newcomer in town, Macy's. And with the consolidation went the multiple ads that had bulked up the *Times* pages.

The troubles of department stores and newspapers had much in common, said Alberto Ibargüen, president of the John S. and James L. Knight Foundation and former publisher of the *Miami Herald*. The stores' "business model assumed that you'd come into the store to buy a shirt, and maybe they'd sell you a tie too, or a suit. The newspaper reels you in to read the sports page, then maybe you take a look at the front page. But the world has changed."

The loss of these advertisers even worried editorial employees, whom Otis had walled off from business concerns. When editors planned the day's paper at the morning news meeting, the editor in charge of allocating space had fewer ads to report. This trend was becoming noticeable at newspapers around the country, and it foreshadowed a precipitous decline in the newspaper business.

Most important, researchers were swiftly combining computer networks into the World Wide Web, which would eventually push newspapers to the brink of obsolescence. News and feature readership began to migrate to the Internet, as did classified and motor-vehicle ads. Neil Kaplan, a former *Times* classified advertising executive, told Mark Lacter of *Los Angeles Magazine*, "There came a time when we looked at each other and came to the realization that the fundamental economic structure of this industry was gone."

The situation was made worse by a number of Times Mirror decisions over the years. The purchase of afternoon papers in Dallas and Denver, at a time when such papers were failing across the country, turned out to be a mistake. The

After prodding public officials to create smog-control agencies, the *Times* continued to publicize the issue with in-depth stories exploring the problem.

company sold several television stations too cheaply. It pulled back from cable and passed up an opportunity to buy a large share of Ted Turner's expanding cable enterprise. In addition, Times Mirror sold its newsprint and forest business, Publishers Paper Co. Several other companies that had been acquired to help diversify Times Mirror and decrease its reliance on the newspaper business were also sold.

To understand what happened to the *Los Angeles Times* in this era of diminishing returns, it's important to take a look at the paper's internal politics. The loss of advertising presented enormous challenges. In addition, there was constant criticism from conservative Chandlers who, as major shareholders, were on the Times Mirror board but not directly involved in the news operation. That side of the family was increasingly alienated from Otis's *Times*.

It was too liberal, too fixated on Pulitzer Prizes, said Tad Williamson, Otis's cousin:

> Eastern intellectuals . . . that's what the Pulitzer Prize committee is, eastern judgments about local papers. And a local paper is satisfying local needs. That wasn't enough for Otis. He wanted national recognition and the only way to get it was to hire people and lead them,

Otis and his good friend John Thomas (right) after a race. Competing at Watkins Glen fulfilled one of his lifelong dreams. TOP: Otis on one of his motorcycles in the Chandler Vintage Museum of Transportation and Wildlife. Along with antique and muscle cars, the collection included prime Harley-Davidsons manufactured over an eighty-year period.

push them, force them to write articles, series that would get the attention of the Pulitzer Prize committee. His measure of the success and worth of the paper was the number of prizes it won.

The family's estrangement was deep. As far as the Chandler cousins were concerned, Williamson said:

> We knew very early on that none of us was going to work at the *Times*. I had no thought of going to work for the *Times*. I can't remember if it was something Mother said or something that I gathered from family communications. But it was pretty clear-cut.

Otis understood the ill will his cousins felt toward him. On top of that, the job of publisher was exhausting him. For several years, he had been talking about stepping down as publisher and moving up to the head of Times Mirror corporate operations, as his father had. He had mentioned this to Thomas when they were on a trip to Spain in 1975. Johnson also remembered hearing Otis say that

> he thought that around the twentieth anniversary of his becoming publisher of the *Times*—sometime around 1980—he would consider moving up in the company and choosing a new publisher. He made it clear I would have a shot at that but in no way was it a guarantee. I worked very, very hard during those years to prove myself.

In addition, Otis said, the stress of the job and pressure from the family was affecting his health:

> My spastic colon was bothering me night and day, I wasn't sleeping very well. I was frankly wearing out with all of the jobs I was doing for the company simultaneously. I was going to the family meetings and having to deal with difficult differences there as to what they wanted for the *Times* versus the way the *Times* was being run. And I was serving on eight or nine corporate boards. I was on an airplane once a week to New York, Chicago, Washington—I was making speeches. I was going twenty-four hours a day.

In 1980, Otis finally took the step. He promoted Johnson to publisher of the *Times* and made himself the paper's editor-in-chief and chairman of Times Mirror. Thomas tried to talk Otis out of stepping

Otis and his second wife, Bettina Whitaker, in 1981, the year they were married.

down as publisher:

> I saw no reason that he had to leave as publisher to be chairman . . . it seemed to me we would lose a bulwark against all outside pressure and also the kind of atmosphere we had between the publisher and the editorial department. But when Tom came in [his] attitude and the workability between the two of us was the same . . .

But Thomas could see Johnson feeling "more pressure as time went on from corporate." In a gloomy foreshadowing of what would happen at the *Times*, Thomas said, "All corporations eventually want to run the place and eventually they all will."

By appointing Johnson, Otis was challenging his cousins and doing it with a certain disdain for the power they held. Given Johnson's closeness to LBJ and their shared liberal values, it was inevitable that Johnson as *Times* publisher would run afoul of the conservative family members.

The family's influence was exercised through trusts created by Harry Chandler. Few people in Los Angeles—even *Times*

Otis Chandler on Spring Street in front of several company vans. LEFT: The troubles on Wall Street in the late 1980s, culminating in the crash of October 1987, affected the Southland's economy and began to hurt *Times* ad revenues.

reporters, who considered themselves in the know—had ever heard of the trusts. But the family members serving on the boards of Chandis Securities Co. and the two Chandler trusts had the real power at Times Mirror and by extension at the *Times*. Otis, one of the trustees, prevented them from interfering with the paper. He was the first among equals on the trust boards as Norman Chandler's designated successor and as a leader who had made the family a great deal of money. "Otis put money in our pockets," said Douglas Goodan, who had served as a Chandis trustee. "He increased the profitability and the business end of the newspaper and the Chandler family participated . . . in that growth of the profits. I think he did a hell of a good job. But nobody appreciates it."

Through the years, Otis protected his staff from all sorts of complaints from family members and from Times Mirror executives. Johnson said that Otis "provided the heat shield behind which we could be independent, and we could report truthfully." Without Otis's protection, pressure on the journalists would have come down from a variety of sources. Buff Chandler objected to the way the distinguished music critic Martin Bernheimer reviewed the Los Angeles Philharmonic. "She would express herself directly to Otis," Johnson said. "But I never had Otis call me and say you go tell Martin Bernheimer I want more favorable coverage of the Music Center. He just didn't do it."

Chandler family members and Times Mirror executives criticized Paul Conrad's political cartoons. Johnson said one person enraged by Conrad was Dr. Franklin Murphy, the former UCLA chancellor who was chairman of Times Mirror. "He would come down to Otis's office with the tear sheet [of Conrad's cartoon] in hand. But to the best of my knowledge, Otis never, never told Paul Conrad he should back off." Another angry Conrad reader

TOP: Meeting of L.A. notables. From left: Tom Johnson, Los Angeles Mayor Tom Bradley, Otis Chandler, and Hugh Hefner. BOTTOM: Cartoonist Paul Conrad (second from right), Tom Johnson (right) and editorial staffers celebrate winning a Pulitzer Prize. OPPOSITE: Otis Chandler talks to *Times* reporters in the newsroom.

Otis Chandler (left) and Tom Johnson enjoyed a close friendship. Here they are overshadowed by a huge stuffed polar bear, one of Otis's many hunting trophies.

was Fred Hartley, the president of Union Oil, who objected to being called "Fred Heartless" in a cartoon showing Union Oil tankers lined up outside Los Angeles harbor, waiting to deliver oil to the refinery, while Southern California endured long gas-station lines. Complaints increased, Johnson said:

> The family members were upset at what they considered the liberal editorial page . . . the family was putting pressure on Otis. They were growing increasingly unhappy about what they considered the liberal direction of the *Times*, first under Otis and then under Tom Johnson . . . They felt we should have been much more conservative.

Another critic was Archbishop (later Cardinal) Roger Mahony, who headed the local Catholic archdiocese. Personally, he could be charming. Politically, he championed a theology of social justice, with emphasis on the growing population of poor Latino immigrants. But when it came to abortion or other aspects of Catholic doctrine, he reacted fiercely and vindictively against other views. *Times* editorials favored women's right to choose abortions. Mahony read the paper every morning and fired off letters to writers, editors, and his friend, Robert Erburu, the chief executive officer of Times Mirror. "Bob was a high-ranking officer of the Catholic Church, had all types of honors," Johnson said. Mahony wrote Erburu that the *Times* was "an ultraliberal newspaper," a message Erburu passed on to Chandler and Johnson. "And Archbishop Mahony sent many messages directly to me," Johnson said. Mahony, interestingly, overlooked the fact that Conrad opposed abortion.

Erburu had come to Times Mirror with F. Daniel Frost, his colleague at the major Los Angeles law firm Gibson, Dunn & Crutcher. Erburu and Frost had been hired by Norman and Dorothy Chandler some twenty years before as personal legal advisers and outside counsel for the expanding Times Mirror Co. Frost married Otis's sister, Camilla, a match that ended in divorce several years later. Erburu left Gibson, Dunn & Crutcher to join Times Mirror. Frost stayed with the law firm. Both accumulated power in Times Mirror. Frost's family connections and formidable legal skill made him a valuable advisor to the Chandlers. As a Times Mirror director, he helped Erburu navigate through the tangle of family relationships and move up in the company hierarchy.

As chairman of Times Mirror, Otis brushed off the family complaints. A witness and participant to all this was Peter Fernald, a Times Mirror vice president who had helped create the diversification program. In his view, Otis

> made a very serious mistake in not building a power base for himself. He was so arrogant, he didn't think he needed a power base. So Bob Erburu was able to staff the board and staff the management to support Bob Erburu. As a result, when push came to shove . . . the only people who stood up for him [Otis] were the journalists. The journalists don't have any votes.

In 1986, Otis's conservative cousins and their allies on the Times Mirror board decided he should go. His biographer, Dennis McDougal, wrote that emissaries from the Times Mirror board, led by Dan Frost, told Otis it was time for him to leave his post as editor-in-chief and chairman of Times Mirror. As Fernald states:

> There was no appeal when they told him to leave. There was no support on the board, in the family, at the company. I think it hurt his pride to be told, especially after his achievement there. Otis did a remarkable job. And he was pensioned.

Otis told family members closest to him that Frost had pushed him into early retirement. Others blamed Frost, Otis's uncle Harrison Chandler, and two of Otis's cousins, Bruce Chandler and Warren "Spud" Williamson. Otis remained on the board, with the title of Chairman of the Executive Committee, but he no longer held any power.

Whoever was to blame, Otis had no idea it was coming. His friend John Thomas remembered the day it happened. Otis called Thomas. Thomas recalled the conversation:

> [Otis] said "I've just been fired . . . I'm no longer the editor-in-

Otis and Bob Erburu having a discussion. Erburu was chief executive officer of Times Mirror when the decision was made to drop Otis from the board.

chief and I'm no longer the head of the board" and he's almost crying, he's almost in tears.. . . . And I said "we're going to meet at Tony's [a restaurant where they often dined] . . . he said "okay." . . . thank God Bettina was with him because I think she even drove.. . . We sat there for two and a half hours and just talked and just let him vent, and he cried, and we all cried. I think he was just totally blindsided . . . He had no idea and all of a sudden—bam!—he was out of a job.

Tom Johnson said of Otis that the dismissal "broke his heart."

Johnson was to be next. The first sign that he had lost Otis's heat shield—and his independence—was an order from the Times Mirror corporate office instructing him to drop the law firm that had long handled *Times* labor relations and replace it with Dan Frost's firm. He said Frost convinced Erburu to do this. Then Otis told Johnson that they could no longer communicate. "Otis told me that he was told by Bob [Erburu] not to have direct contact with me anymore" and that Johnson himself should deal only with Phil Williams, one of Erburu's top lieutenants. Amid the pressure, Johnson suffered from episodes of severe depression when well-concealed inner demons surfaced, driving him to the verge of suicide. "My mood is really low," he wrote one Sunday during this period. "Feel trapped. Often I think of 'checking out.'"

The final blow came on March 21, 1989, when Johnson was ordered to fire the editor of the editorial pages, Anthony Day, who

had been hired by Otis Chandler years before. Day and Otis were the architects of the page, shaping it as a moderate voice with a liberal leaning on social issues. For the most part, the editorials were in the middle of the ideological spectrum.

Johnson refused the order. "I was proud of the editorial pages of the *Los Angeles Times*," Johnson said. "I was proud of Tony Day and the people he had. When word came down to me that I should fire Tony Day, I said absolutely 'No; in fact, hell no.'" Even though he had complained about Conrad's cartoons, Dr. Murphy, then the chairman of Times Mirror, came to Johnson's

ABOVE: Tom Johnson. OPPOSITE: Robert Erburu, president of Times Mirror Co. (left); Dr. Franklin Murphy, chairman of the executive committee, and Otis were firmly in charge at the beginning of the 1980s. By the end of the decade, the team broke up as economic troubles hit the company.

office to commiserate. He told Johnson, "Certain family members and leaders in the business and religious community consider Day ultraliberal . . . I would not fire Tony Day, either." Johnson said, "As a former chancellor at UCLA, Franklin understood the value of academic and journalistic independence, although he too was often upset with the *Times'* editorial pages and with Paul Conrad's cartoons."

One of the business leaders, Howard Allen, chairman of Southern California Edison, invited Johnson to lunch. Johnson

Tom Johnson (right) at a meeting with Jack Nelson, chief of the *Times* Washington bureau.

says that Allen disliked *Times* editorials favoring anti-pollution measures and expressing concern about Edison's nuclear power plant on the coast at San Onofre.

As Johnson recalls it, Allen told him, "Tom, either you start running the *Times* the way Dan Frost and the Chandler family want it run or you will be out as publisher."

Despite the pressure, Johnson stuck by Day. In 1989, the Times Mirror board of directors removed Johnson as publisher and offered him a demeaning job in the corporate hierarchy. Less than a year later, he quit and accepted Ted Turner's offer to head CNN. Day was removed as editorial page editor and became a writer for the paper.

In a letter to Johnson a decade later, Otis wrote:

> I tried to use whatever power I had as a director and chairman of the executive committee to keep you on as publisher, and after they acted on your removal as publisher to put you in a top corporate job, but I failed—I had lost my power base . . . The whole event was sad and depressing for me and awful for you. You didn't deserve what happened to you.

Otis Chandler and Tom Johnson presided over the greatest years of the *Times*. When their era ended, the paper was regarded as one of the country's top three. In part, they were beaten by Chandler family politics. But the paper's problems were much bigger than that. Economic tides supporting the industry had shifted. Readers were turning elsewhere for their news, and advertisers were using new media to reach consumers. In addition, Southern California—initially stirred into growth and shaped by the Chandlers themselves—had grown beyond the paper's ability to influence or even cover such a huge, sprawling and diverse area.

This was a job that would have taxed the skills of an Otis Chandler or a Tom Johnson, and certainly was far beyond the capacities of their successors. The Los Angeles the Chandlers had built would, of course, continue, even grow. But with the last of the Chandlers—as well as Otis's designated successor—gone, the paper's economic health was in question. Unbelievably, so was its survival.

"Just as Harrison Gray Otis used his newspaper to promote the rise of Los Angeles from a remote western town to an important American metropolis, Otis Chandler, during his watch on the *Times*, helped Los Angeles move towards international prominence, helped it become a world city." —Kevin Starr

EQVAL RIGHTS

TRVE INDVSTRIAL FREEDOM

· THIS · STONE · WAS · SET ·
· THIS · DAY · APRIL · 10 · 1934
· BY · HARRY · CHANDLER
· PUBLISHER · OF · THE ·
· LOS · ANGELES · TIMES

The Chandler Era Ends

Most of the time, workers on the factory floor can't explain why their company failed. By necessity, their view doesn't extend much beyond the car they are assembling or the supervisor giving them orders. A newspaper, however, is a different kind of manufacturing plant. A number of the workers are journalists, often high-strung creatures, trained to observe every nuance, rumor, and fact. At the *Los Angeles Times*, the journalists' factory floor—the newsroom—was the best place to observe the sad final decade of Chandler control.

The newsroom, on the third floor, extends the length of a long city block, from one end of the *Los Angeles Times* building to the other. In 1989, the year Tom Johnson was fired as publisher, the many departments in the room reflected the ambitions of a paper at its height. Books, Fashion, Food, Calendar (covering movies, television, art, and music) occupied one large portion

This bronze statue of General Harrison Gray Otis stands in a corner of MacArthur Park, near his former home. Next to him is a second, smaller statue of a newsboy. PAGES 190-191: TOP: Downtown Los Angeles today, with its cluster of high-rises framed against the snow-covered San Gabriel Mountains. PAGE 190 BOTTOM: The cornerstone of the new home of the *Los Angeles Times*, which was built in 1934 about a block from the original structure. The cornerstone was of polished California black granite and weighed three and a half tons. It contained a copper box of mementos, including some from the earlier building's cornerstone. PAGE 191 BOTTOM: The present-day *Los Angeles Times* building at dawn.

of the room, blending into Sports, and then Business. Near Business were the foreign and national desks, receiving stories from bureaus around the country and the world. Beyond these desks was the Metro staff, covering local news, and then there were the specialists in education, science, medicine, religion and the environment.

Each day, at 10 A.M. and 2:30 P.M., their work went on display in a conference room. There, the editors in charge of the sections discussed which stories and pictures to run and where to place them. They would pick a few for page one and consign others to the many inside pages of the paper. The meetings were a daily presentation of events around the world, ranging from violence in the Middle East to a vote in Congress to a mishap on Santa Monica Beach, interspersed with a mix of movies, art, music, sports, food, and literature. Even with Otis Chandler gone, the choices still reflected his philosophy of "mass and class."

As the 1980s ended, and Chandler and Johnson were driven from power, the journalists in the newsroom were uneasy. The paper was adrift. They had a new publisher, David Laventhol. Another unknown quantity, Shelby Coffey III, was editor, replacing Bill Thomas, who retired in 1989. Upstairs, the conservative Chandlers were in firm control of the board and were more determined than ever to revive the legacy of Harry Chandler—and make a lot of money while doing it. They found support in the Times Mirror hierarchy, now under the firm control of Robert Erburu.

Ideology was no longer an issue. With Tony Day gone, the conservatives had won and objections to a liberal editorial slant had faded. The editorial pages became bland. The editorial board's lively discussions of issues, which had largely shaped the editorials, were abandoned. The great liberal cartoonist, Paul Conrad, left the paper in 1993, replaced by a conservative, Michael Ramirez.

Now the main pressure was economic. The *Los Angeles Business Journal* had reported in 1991 that after two years of declining earnings, Times Mirror projected a loss in the fourth quarter. Company executives said the editorial department was fat and wasteful.

The atmosphere grew even more unsettling when Laventhol, the new publisher, instituted some cost-cutting measures, including elimination of first-class air travel. Rumors swept through the newsroom. The rebellious nature of the staff—a hangover from the journalists Thomas had hired and nurtured—heightened the staff's sense of apprehension.

Despite all the newsroom gossip and speculation, workers were generally ignorant of the corporation's financial situation and strategic plan. The wall that Otis Chandler had erected between business operations and the editorial department had been so effective that the reporters felt themselves immune from what was happening in the corporate offices on the sixth floor. They were, in fact, scornful of those who worked on the paper's business side. The vast majority of editors were just as ignorant as the reporters. The few who knew what was happening didn't choose to share their knowledge.

Thomas's successor, Coffey, was a slender, athletic man who had bonded with Otis Chandler a few years before when they were lifting weights in a Washington gym. Johnson had chosen him as editor after a dragged-out process that required Coffey, who had been editor of the Dallas *Times Herald*, and the other contenders for the job to write essays laying out their plans for the paper.

Thomas had made him a deputy associate editor in the features department, but it was clear he was on his way to bigger things. Even though his mandate was features, he went out to lunch with editors in the hard news departments and asked questions about what they did and the difficulties they faced in their coverage.

Once established as editor, Coffey could be an excellent and exciting leader. For example, he loved the O.J. Simpson murder trial and often wandered to the section of the newsroom where the O.J. team worked to talk about the event. But he was cautious and often reluctant to take a chance on a daring idea. His editors sensed his reluctance and copied it.

Nor did Coffey or his editors know how to deal with a changing Southland. The model that Otis Chandler had created, essentially aimed at middle-class Southern Californians who got their information by reading, was no longer viable. The paper's suburban sections were not attracting advertisers, and the large Orange County and San Fernando Valley editions were steadily losing ground.

The *Times* trailed competitors in seven of eleven Southern California market areas. Various attempts were made to turn things around, but nothing seemed to work. The San Fernando Valley and Orange County editions were turned into virtually independent papers, putting local stories from their areas on page one. The Otis Chandler formula, stressing the importance of national and foreign stories, was abandoned. Orange County, especially, consumed so many resources that it became known as the *Times'* Vietnam, a quagmire with no victory in sight. On top of this, the readers and advertisers continued to drift away.

In 1995, as revenues continued to fall, the Chandler family reached outside Times Mirror and brought in an outsider as president and CEO of Times Mirror. Mark Willes, as vice-president of General Mills was known as "Cap'n Crunch" because of his reputation as a marketer with a focus on cost cutting and the bottom line. Two years after becoming CEO, Willes appointed himself publisher of the *Times*. He held the two jobs until 1999 when he appointed a new publisher, his protégé Kathryn Downing, who had headed another Times Mirror company. Whatever the titles, Willes was in command.

Unlike Tom Johnson or Otis Chandler, who both had left control of the newsroom to the editor, Willes was eager to meet reporters and ask about their work. Sometimes he invited them to lunch in the executive dining room. The reporters were surprised and flattered by the attention. In his public speeches, he spoke emotionally and cried when the subject—or his words—moved him. At first, audiences were impressed by this rare show of male emotion, but some people felt it was an act after seeing him cry on more than one occasion. The writers he courted began to question whether his tears and his concern for their work were an essential part of the Willes act.

Willes shut down the network of suburban editions except for the San Fernando Valley and Orange County editions. Editors were shifted around. Two Times Mirror newspapers, *New York Newsday* and the *Baltimore Evening Sun*, were closed. The payroll was reduced by a thousand jobs, with the *Times* hit hardest. Coffey looked gray and stricken the day he announced the cuts.

Willes's most controversial change was to break down the figurative wall between the editorial department and the business side, mainly advertising. Otis Chandler had separated these departments to prevent advertisers from dictating the content of news stories, the way things had been done at newspapers in the past. Willes challenged the concept, saying he would use a bazooka to blow up the wall. He saw the editorial department as recalcitrant in its resistance to this change. Although he continued to have reporters to lunch, he couldn't understand why they didn't support his agenda. He felt the entire paper should unite behind him and help reach his goal of more advertising, circulation, and revenue. The journalists shared those goals, but they also regarded their business as a calling. Their primary goal was to dig out the news, not help sell ads.

To bring the journalists to heel, he installed mini-publishers in each of the editorial departments to work with the editors and come up with new ways of selling ads. The arrival of the mini-publishers soured the newsroom even more. So did troubling incidents, such as the advertising chief's nearly successful attempt to have the consumer columnist fired when he exposed the fraudulent auto sales tactics of a major advertiser.

Uncertainty became a way of life in the newsroom. Sensing the disaster ahead, Coffey had resigned when Willes named himself publisher. The new editor was Michael Parks, a Pulitzer Prize-winning foreign correspondent who had been managing editor. He had been a reporter for most of his career. He appreciated reporters and stood behind them when their stories were attacked by such powers as the mayor or the chief of police. He didn't know much about management, but even the best of managers would have had trouble surviving this chaotic situation.

Parks tried to compromise when he was hit by orders from Willes and Downing that conflicted with the needs of his nervous staff. Editors grew frightened. They learned a new skill: managing up. It was a phrase beloved by management gurus, but in the newsroom it translated into the bowing and groveling of lower-level editors trying to please the layers of bosses above them. They second-guessed story ideas and turned down any that might displease management. Assignments came from the top down. Completed stories went through the hands of several editors. It was no longer a writer's newspaper.

Willes and Downing charged ahead in their determination to win more advertising. A big new privately financed arena, the Staples Center, was nearing completion in downtown Los Angeles. The arena owners were seeking "founding partners" to help defray construction costs. Without divulging the plan to its editorial staff, management at the *Times* enrolled the paper as a founding partner of Staples Center at a cost of $1.8 million a year for five years. They also agreed to produce an edition of the *Times* Sunday magazine celebrating the opening of the arena. The paper and the new arena would share the advertising profits from this issue of the magazine. The arena management solicited its vendors and contractors to buy ads.

The secret arrangement was disclosed in local weekly papers and then in stories in the *New York Times* and the *Wall Street Journal.* The *Journal* said the arrangement "raised serious questions about how far a paper can go without damaging its integrity."

The national headlines touched off a rebellion in the newsroom at the *Los Angeles Times.* A petition was circulated demanding an apology from Downing. The next day, Downing met with the staff in the company cafeteria, filled beyond capacity. For ninety minutes, she faced unrelenting, belligerent questioning. She apologized "to each of you . . . To have the *New York Times,* the *Wall Street Journal* or anyone for that matter question our integrity is a horrendous place to be, and I am responsible for that."

Otis Chandler watched all this from his ranch in Ojai. He had grown skeptical of Willes. "The *Times* is at great risk I think being run by people who have good intentions, are smart and so on, but no experience," he said. "I think there's a vulnerability."

But Chandler no longer had any power at the *Times*. In 1998, he had been dropped from the board after he expressed his feelings about the family to journalist David Margolick for a 1996 profile in *Vanity Fair*. Margolick quoted him saying his relatives were "coupon clippers . . . elitists . . . bored with the problems of AIDS and the homeless and drive-by shootings." He was not even offered the choice of staying on as a non-voting director, a gesture often offered to other board members.

There were no longer any Chandlers on the staff of the *Los Angeles Times*. Otis's oldest son, Norman, had undergone the same training program as his father and, like Otis, particularly enjoyed his work as a reporter. He learned how to cover the news, was intelligent, seemed to have the spark of leadership, and was popular with his co-workers. But Otis didn't think Norman merited high command in the company:

> The Chandler family would not have accepted Norman as publisher. He is not an outgoing, tough, aggressive leader as I was. He had no leadership jobs through the years as I did. He wasn't in the service. He's . . . gracious and kind . . . [but] if they put him in he would have failed because it wasn't meant to be.

The issue was moot. Norman was discovered to have an inoperable brain tumor and died after a long decline.

His other son, Harry, was also interested in coming into the company, but his father didn't offer him the opportunity for executive training that Norman had experienced. Harry finally went to work at the *Times* in its new media area. "I joined without him making a phone call," Harry said. But he said Willes wasn't interested in new media. "And I think as a Chandler, Mark Willes didn't feel like [I was] his best friend . . ." But even if Otis had been the pushiest of fathers, the family members controlling the board never would have given power to his sons. The Chandler era was just about over.

After the Staples scandal broke, Otis brooded at his ranch. Then he wrote a long message to the editorial department. He placed a call to the city editor, one of the few staff members he still knew, and asked him to deliver the message to the staff. The city editor, seated at his computer, took it down.

Otis read his remarks over the phone, with words reflecting his fury and sorrow:

> To the employees of the *Los Angeles Times*, particularly of the editorial department because they have been so abused and misused . . . [by] the downsizing of the *Times* . . . the shrinking of the *Times* in terms of employees . . . the ill-advised steps that have been taken by current management . . . breaking down barriers, the traditional wall between editorial and the business departments.
>
> My heart is heavy, my emotions are indescribable because I am afraid I am witnessing now a period in time in the history of this newspaper that is beyond description . . . I applaud the efforts of individual reporters who have spoken openly at their recent meeting with Kathryn Downing, and I also heartily endorse the letter that was presented to Michael Parks on November 2 which calls for a full and impartial publishing of all of the events that led up to the Staples controversy . . .
>
> If a newspaper, even a great newspaper like the *Los Angeles Times*, loses credibility with its community, with its readers, with its advertisers, with its shareholders, that is probably the most serious circumstance that I can possibly think of. Respect and

credibility of a newspaper is irreplaceable. Sometimes it never can be restored no matter what steps might be taken in terms of apology by the publisher, apology by the head of Times Mirror or whatever post-event strategies might be developed in the hopes of putting the pieces back together.

When I think back through the history . . . of this great newspaper . . . I realize how fragile and irreplaceable public trust in a newspaper is. This public trust and faith in a newspaper by its employees, its readers, the community, is dearer to me than life itself.

At six o'clock that evening, after the paper's deadline, the city editor called the entire staff together and read Otis's words to a packed newsroom. There was silence while the message was read, followed by applause. Soon after, pictures of Otis were posted throughout the big room.

Downing called Otis "angry and bitter." Somewhat surprisingly, his foes in the family were resentful of her statement—who was *she* to insult a Chandler? Even before the Staples scandal, the family had been considering selling Times Mirror. Willes had pretty much stripped the company down to its print enterprises, and it was clear by 2000 that the newspaper business was heading downhill. Downing's insult to Otis and the intensive national coverage of the Staples controversy gave the family a final push toward concluding the sale. On March 13, 2000, Times Mirror became part of the company that owned the Chicago Tribune.

Otis said he was pleased that the Tribune Company was taking over. A few weeks later, he and Bettina returned to the paper for the first time since he had been dismissed from the board. With Bettina at his side, he walked through the entire newsroom, past the pictures of him still hanging there. He stopped at every department. The journalists crowded around him, wanting to greet him. Many were meeting him for the first time.

He had brought integrity, honor and civic responsibility to the *Los Angeles Times* as well as great prosperity. Aware of what he had given to the paper—and knowing those days were passing—the workers on the newsroom floor were proud to shake his hand.

OPPOSITE: Long retired, Otis Chandler occasionally visited the paper after Times Mirror was sold to the Tribune Company. Behind him is an exhibit of the newspaper's history.

Acknowledgments

It's an understatement to say that many people helped me with this book. Los Angeles and Southern California history, while short by world or even American standards, is so rich, scandalous, and convoluted that it has attracted many historians, who produced uncounted books and articles about the Southland. I've read many of them and couldn't have written this book without their work.

First of all, thanks to Nancy Boyarsky, my wife, and an invaluable collaborator on this book. As a skilled and experienced editor, she helped organize the material and edited the book line by line before it went to Angel City Press. She also wrote the captions and helped with the picture selection. As someone who has shared my good days and bad at the *Los Angeles Times*, she had sharp insights on many of the characters in the book.

Two books on the *Times* were invaluable. The first is *Thinking Big: The Story of the Los Angeles Times, Its Publishers and Their Influence on Southern California* by Robert Gottlieb and Irene Wolt. The other is Dennis McDougal's *Privileged Son: Otis Chandler and the Rise and Fall of the L.A. Times Dynasty*.

In his multi-volume history of California, Kevin Starr focuses much attention on the Southland's cultural life, as well as its politics, people, and public works. I thought I knew a lot, but he broadened my view. And, of course, thanks to the great chronicler of California, the late Carey McWilliams—whose writings help teach me that journalism is more than news stories.

My colleague Kevin Roderick, contributed to my education with his book *The San Fernando Valley: America's Suburb*. I consulted the works of other authors who are in the bibliography. But I'd like to give a special mention to historian Ann Gorman Condon. She edited *Architects of Our Fortunes: The Journal of Eliza A.W. Otis, 1860-1863, with Letters and Civil War Journal of Harrison Gray Otis*. She showed that the shouting old warhorse of a publisher had a human side.

Thanks also to Peter Jones, the producer of the documentary *Inventing Los Angeles*, upon which this book is based. His film provided the structure of this book and the story of the *Times* publishers. He obtained the pictures, without which there would have been no film or book. He provided me with volumes of interviews he used in his documentary, material that has never been published, as well as unpublished Chandler documents and memos he had gathered. It was also great sharing Chandler stories with him, balancing my impressions against his. My special thanks to Mark Catalena and Brian Tessier of Peter Jones Productions, who edited the images which help to tell the story of the Chandlers and their *Times*.

Finally, thanks to Angel City Press and its publishers Paddy Calistro and Scott McAuley, and graphic designer Amy Inouye. They combined the text and pictures to create a real addition to the literature of Los Angeles history.

—BB

Photography Credits

The author, photography editors, and publisher thank the following individuals and institutions for the use of images in *Inventing L.A.: The Chandlers and Their Times*. Every effort has been made to correctly identify the source of each image. Please notify the publisher of any errors or omissions.

Autry National Center/Southwest Museum: 72 (right).

California Historical Society Digital Archive, University of Southern California: 53, 62-63, 96-97.

The California State Library: 12-13.

Mark Catalena/Peter Jones Productions: 190, 191, 192.

Chandler Family Archives: Endpapers (Norman and Otis Chandler), 102, 104, 106, 108, 117, 119, 122-124, 128, 129 (right), 130, 142 (left and center), 143 (top), 154-155, 159, 162, 163 (left), 171, 179, 180, 181 (right), 184, 186, 199.

Cleveland Public Library: 57.

The Huntington Library: Cover, endpapers (except where otherwise noted), 3, 14, 15-16, 19, 23, 25-27, 29-31, 33 (top), 36-37, 41, 44-48, 51-52, 54-56, 59, 61, 68-70, 75-76, 78-79, 81 (top), 82, 95, 100-101, 107, 109, 111, 118, 121, 125, 127, 136-138, 140, 142 (right), 143 (bottom), 148-150, 151 (left), 153, 158, 160-161, 164-165, 167-170, 172-174, 177, 182, 183 (top), 185, 187.

Library of Congress: 20.

The Lilly Library, Indiana University, Bloomington, Indiana: 92.

Los Angeles Department of Water and Power: 38.

Los Angeles Times Collection/UCLA Library Special Collections: 2, 6, 64-65, 66-67, 68-70, 72 (left), 91, 94, 98-99, 103, 113 (top), 132-135, 144, 146, 183 (bottom), 188.

Los Angeles Public Library: Endpapers (Los Angeles Times building, second row), 39, 73, 88, 90, 115.

Los Angeles Times Reprints. 4, 22, 28, 32, 41, 50, 80, 112, 113 (bottom), 129 (left), 145, 151 (right), 156-157, 178, 181 (left).

Ernest Marquez: 87.

The Museum of the San Fernando Valley: 83, 85.

The Music Center Archives: 131.

National Japanese American Historical Society: 114.

Peter Jones Productions Archives: 21, 24, 42-43.

San Pedro Bay Historical Society: 33 (bottom), 34.

Seaver Center for Western History Research, Natural History of Museum of Los Angeles County: 40, 79 (bottom), 84.

Larry Strayer: 18.

University of Cincinnati Archives and Rare Books Library: 58.

Wall Street Journal Archives: 163 (right).

Jon Wilkman: 10-11.

Bibliography

Casey, Al. *Casey's Law: If Something Can Go Right, It Should.* New York: Arcade Publishing, 1997.

Condon, Ann Gorman. *Architects of Our Fortunes: The Journal of Eliza A.W. Otis, 1860-1863, with Letters and Civil War Journal of Harrison Gray Otis.* San Marino, California: Huntington Library Press, 2001.

Cowan, Geoffrey. *The People v. Clarence Darrow: The Bribery Trial of America's Greatest Lawyer.* New York: Times Books, Random House, 1993.

Estrada, William D. *Los Angeles's Olvera Street.* Chicago: Arcadia Publishing, 2006.

Fradkin, Philip L. *The Seven States of California: A Natural and Human History.* Berkeley: University of California Press, 1997.

Gottlieb, Robert. *A Life of Its Own: The Politics and Power of Water.* San Diego, New York: Harcourt Brace Javonovich, 1988.

Gottlieb, Robert and Irene Wolt. *Thinking Big: The Story of the Los Angeles Times, Its Publishers and Their Influence on Southern California.* Berkeley : University of California Press, 1979.

Greenwald, Marilyn and Joseph Bernt [eds.]. *The Big Chill: Investigative Reporting in the Current Media Environment.* Ames, IA: Iowa State University Press, 2000.

Leonard, Kevin Allen. *The Battle for Los Angeles: Racial Ideology and World War II.* Albuquerque: University of New Mexico Press, 2006.

Marquez, Ernest, and Veronique de Turenne. *Port of Los Angeles: An Illustrated History from 1850 to 1945.* Santa Monica: Angel City Press, 2007.

McDougal, Dennis. *Privileged Son: Otis Chandler and the Rise and Fall of the L.A. Times Dynasty.* Cambridge, Massachusetts: Perseus Publishing, 2001.

McWilliams, Carey. *Southern California: An Island on the Land.* Santa Barbara: Gibbs Smith, 1973.

Mitchell, Greg. *The Campaign of the Century: Upton Sinclair's Race for Governor of California and the Birth of Media Politics.* New York: Random House, 1992.

Pitt, Leonard, and Dale Pitt. *Los Angeles A to Z: An Encyclopedia of the City and County.* Berkeley: University of California Press, 1997.

Reisner, Marc. *Cadillac Desert.* New York: Viking Penguin, 1986.

Robinson, W.W. *Lawyers of Los Angeles.* Los Angeles: Los Angeles County Bar Association, 1959.

Roderick, Kevin. *The San Fernando Valley: America's Suburb.* Los Angeles: Los Angeles Times Books, 2001.

—. *Wilshire Boulevard: Grand Concourse of Los Angeles.* Santa Monica: Angel City Press, 2005.

Shaffer, Ralph E. *Letters from the People:* Los Angeles Times, *1881-1889.* Pomona, California: Department of History, California State Polytechnic University, Pomona, 1999. http://www.csupomona.edu/~reshaffer/

Starr, Kevin. *Endangered Dreams: The Great Depression in California.* New York: Oxford University Press, 1996.

—. *Material Dreams: Southern California Through the 1920s.* New York: Oxford University Press, 1990.

Steffens, Lincoln. *The Autobiography of Lincoln Steffens.* Berkeley: Heyday Books, 1931.

Tygiel, Jules. *The Great Los Angeles Swindle: Oil, Stocks, and Scandal During the Roaring Twenties.* Berkeley: University of California Press, 1996.

Weaver, John D. *Los Angeles: The Enormous Village, 1781-1981.* Santa Barbara: Capra Press, 1980.

Zimmerman, Tom. *Paradise Promoted: The Booster Campaign That Created Los Angeles 1870-1930.* Santa Monica: Angel City Press, 2008.

ARTICLES AND WEB SITES:

[]. "Public Housing and the Brooklyn Dodgers: Double Play by City Hall in the Ravine." *Frontier* magazine, June 1957.

[]. "The Midwinter Number." *Los Angeles Times*, 1/01/1925.

[]. "The New World." *Time* magazine, 7/15/1957.

[]. "Unionist Bombs Wreck the Times; Many Seriously Injured." *Los Angeles Times*, 10/10/1910.

[]. "Timeline: Zoot Suit Riots." *American Experience* (WGBH). http://www.pbs.org/wgbh/amex/zoot/eng_timeline/index.html

[]. "Los Angeles Zoot Suit Riots." *Los Angeles Almanac.* http://www.laalmanac.com/history/hi07t.htm

Chandler, Harry. "Harry Chandler, 'Oldest Employee,' Has Seen This City Transformed." *Los Angeles Times*, 12/04/1941.

Chandler, Norman. "The Publisher's Opinion: The Value of Optimism." *Los Angeles Times*, 5/25/1959.

Ernst, Brian C. "Joseph Scott: Upholder of American Justice in Los Angeles." The Leavey Center for the Study of Los Angeles, 2003.

Hall, Chapin. "Trade Talk." *Los Angeles Times*, 7/22/1920.

Himstedt, Lucy. "CNN's Tom Johnson: 1999 Paul White Award Recipient." *Communicator* (Radio-Television News Directors Association), September 1999.

Lacter, Mark. "Paper Money." *Los Angeles* magazine, June 2009.

Libby, Joseph E. "To Build Wings for the Angels: Los Angeles and Its Aircraft Industry, 1890-1936." *Business and Economic History*, 1992 Second Series, Vol. 21.

Mollenkamp, Carrick. "Executive's Long Career Is Marked by Depression." *Wall Street Journal Online*, 8/06/2002. http://208.144.115.170/myc/survive/20020806-mollenkamp2.html

Morrison, Patt. "A Prince Who Earned His Crown." *Los Angeles Times*, 2/28/2006.

Shaw, David and Mitchell Landsberg. "A Lion of Journalism." *Los Angeles Times*, 2/28/2006.

Smillie, Dirk. "Can This Man Save the Newspaper Business?" *Forbes.com*, 6/2/2009.

INTERVIEWS:

[]. Interview of Nick Williams (7/08/1981).

Bassett, James. Interview of Norman and Dorothy Chandler.

Jones, Peter. Interview of Camilla Frost (8/10/2006).

—. Interview of Marilyn Brant (8/14/2006).

—. Interview of Peter Fernald (8/17/2006).

Klass, Anita. Interview of Dorothy Chandler (1/15/1980).

Leffingwell, Randy. Interview of Otis Chandler (1998).

Index

Allen, Howard, 188

American Civil Liberties Union, 91

Andrews, Harry E., 53

Angelus Temple, 86

ARCO, 176

Armstrong, Robert B., 77, 78, 93

Atlanta Journal and Constitution, 144

Bernheimer, Martin, 183

Bernstein, Harry, 151

bombing of the *Los Angeles Times,* 27, 49, 50, 53, 54, 55, 57, 59, 90

Booth, Otis, 53, 60

Boston Globe, 144

Bowron, Fletcher, 112

Boyce, Henry, 26

Brant, Otto, 142

Buffums, 109

Burke, Jack, 162

Burke, Marian, 109

Burns, William, 55

California Company, 74

California Institute of Technology, 80, 95

Calle de Los Negros, 22

Casey, Al, 176

Chandis Securities, 159, 183

Chandler, Bruce, 185

Chandler, Carolyn, 154, 159

Chandler, Cathleen, 154, 159

Chandler, Dorothy Buffum, 17, 68, 74, 78, 93, 94, 102, 105, 106, 107, 109, 110, 118, 119, 122, 124, 125, 126, 129, 130, 139, 146, 147, 149, 165, 166, 183, 184, 206

Chandler, Emma, 206

Chandler, Harrison, 107, 159, 185

Chandler, Harry, 8, 17, 24, 25, 26, 31, 35, 36, 41, 53, 59, 60, 61, 64, 68, 71, 72, 74, 75, 77, 78, 79, 81, 84, 85, 86, 89, 90, 92, 94, 95, 105, 107, 120, 142, 146, 152, 154, 158, 159, 176, 183, 194

Chandler, Harry Brant, 154, 159, 197

Chandler, Moses, 206

Chandler, Norman, 8, 9, 17, 40, 60, 72, 93, 94, 95, 98, 100, 105, 106, 107, 109, 110, 111, 117, 118, 120, 122, 123, 124, 125, 139, 141, 143, 144, 145, 146, 147, 149, 150, 151, 158, 161, 165, 183, 184,206

Chandler, Norman (son of Otis), 154, 159, 197

Chandler, Otis, 8, 9, 109, 125, 126, 130, 134, 139, 140, 141, 145, 149, 150, 152, 153, 154, 155, 158, 159, 161, 162, 163, 166, 167, 172, 175, 176, 177, 181, 183, 184, 187, 189, 190, 194, 195, 196, 197, 198, 200

Chandler, Otis Yeager, 154

Chandler, Philip, 107, 125, 126, 144, 146, 151, 159

Chandler, Ralph, 78

Chicago Tribune, 144, 198

Civil War, 17, 18, 20, 28, 200

Clemens, Samuel ("Mark Twain"), 19

Coffey, Shelby III, 194

Condon, Ann Gordon, 19

Congress of Industrial Organizations (C.I.O.), 117

Conrad, Paul, 110, 152, 154, 183, 184, 188, 194

Cowan, Geoffrey, 54

Criminal Syndicalism Act of 1919, 90

Darrow, Clarence, 57

Daugherty, Edward Michael, 89

Day, Anthony, 141, 187, 188, 194

DeYoung, Marilyn Brant "Missy" Chandler, 110, 137, 142, 154

Doheny, Edward L., 18, 25

Douglas, Donald, 74, 80

Downing, Kathryn, 195, 196, 197

Eaton, Fred, 35

Eisenhower, Dwight D., 122, 123, 157

End Poverty in California (EPIC), 91, 92, 93, 94

Erburu, Robert, 165, 176, 184, 185, 187, 194

Fernald, Peter, 165, 185

Frost, F. Daniel, 184

Garland, William, 77

Gibson, Dunn & Crutcher, 184

Gompers, Samuel, 57

Goodan, Douglas, 183

Goodan, May, 159, 161

Goodyear Tire and Rubber, 84

Grand Army Journal, 21

Halberstam, David, 17, 123

Harriman, Job, 57, 59

Hartley, Fred, 184

Hayes, Rutherford B., 21

Henry, Bill, 74

Hollister, W.W., 21

Hollywood Bowl, 126, 129

Hoover, Herbert, 93

Hughes, Howard, 166

Huntington, Collis P., 31, 32

Huntington, Henry, 77, 80

International Association of Bridge and Structural Iron Workers, 54

Jet Propulsion Laboratory, 95

John Birch Society, 151

Johnson, Hiram, 18

Johnson, Tom, 100, 132, 167, 175, 176, 177, 183, 184, 187, 188, 189, 194, 195

Jones, Alex, 134

Julian Petroleum Company, 86

Julian, C.C., 86, 162

Kennedy, John F., 124, 152

La Opinion, 116

Laventhol, David, 194

Lincoln Steffens, 59

Lincoln, Abraham, 20

Los Angeles Chamber of Commerce, 28, 35, 57, 90, 91, 106

Los Angeles City Council, 50, 54

Los Angeles City Water Company, 35

Los Angeles Daily News, 113, 144, 147

Los Angeles Daily Times, 17, 22, 28

Los Angeles Examiner, 37, 110, 113, 147, 150, 151, 152

Los Angeles Herald, 25, 50

Los Angeles Herald-Examiner, 150

Los Angeles Herald-Express, 113, 147

Los Angeles Mirror / Mirror-News, 105, 120, 123, 144, 145, 150, 152, 154, 156, 166

Los Angeles Police Department, 50, 90, 91

Los Angeles Riots, 90

Los Angeles River, 32, 116

Los Angeles Steamship Company, 78

Los Angeles Suburban Homes Company, 59, 85

Los Angeles *Tribune*, 26

Louisville *Journal*, 20

Lummis, Charles Fletcher, 28

Mahony, Roger, 184

Margolick, David, 197

Martin, Glenn, 74

McDougal, Dennis, 89, 185, 200

McFarland, Peter Clark, 28

McKinley, William, 21, 27

McManigal, Ortie, 55

McNamara, James, 54, 55, 57, 59, 60

McNamara, John J., 54, 55, 57, 59, 60

McPherson, Aimee Semple, 86

McWilliams, Carey, 18, 59, 66, 200

Merchants and Manufacturers Association, 50, 54, 91

Merriam, Frank F., 93

Millikan, Robert, 80

Mitchell, Greg, 94

Morrison, Patt, 141

Mulholland, William, 35, 36, 38

Murphy, Franklin, 165, 183, 187

Murray, Jim, 154

Murray, Philip, 117

Music Center, 105, 126, 129, 130, 140, 183

New York Times, 143, 168, 196, 197

Nixon, Richard M., 8, 123, 124, 152, 165

O'Melveny, Henry, 23

Oakland Tribune, 9, 93

Ohio Statesman, 21

Otis, Eliza, 10

Owens Valley, 8, 32, 35, 36, 37, 38, 41, 59, 77, 86, 113

Pacific Electric, 73, 80, 83

Palmer, Kyle, 8, 93, 94, 95, 114, 123, 141

Parks, Michael, 196, 197

Pearl Harbor, 113, 114

Pulitzer Prize, 110, 154, 156, 157, 179, 180, 183, 196

Reagan, Ronald M., 154

Roderick, Kevin, 40, 86, 200

Roosevelt, Eleanor, 117

Roosevelt, Franklin D., 92, 94, 95, 113, 117

Roosevelt, Theodore, 38

Rutten, Tim, 170

San Fernando Mission Land Co., 86

San Fernando Valley, 35, 37, 38, 40, 41, 59, 60, 71, 73, 83, 84, 85, 86, 158, 177, 195, 200

San Francisco Chronicle, 93

San Francisquito Canyon, 40

Santa Barbara Weekly Press, 19

Sargent, Aaron, 21

Saturday Evening Post, 78

Schlador, Magdalena, 25, 26

Scott, Joseph, 57, 60

Security Pacific Bank, 176

Sherman, Moses, 35, 36, 37, 78, 89

Sinclair, Upton, 91, 92, 123

Sleepy Lagoon murder, 115, 117, 120

Southern California Edison, 188

Southern Pacific Railroad, 21, 22, 23, 31, 32

Spanish-American War, 18, 27

Stanford University, 107, 126, 141, 142, 143, 162

Staples Center, 196

Starr, Kevin, 15, 35, 190, 200

Storke, Thomas, 22

Thomas, Bill, 120, 150, 156, 166, 194

Thomas, John, 179, 185

Tournament of Roses, 17

Turner, Ted, 179, 188

Twelfth Ohio Volunteers, 18

UCLA, 165, 166, 183, 188

Union Oil, 176, 184

University of Southern California, 77, 118

Van Nuys, 60, 85, 86

Four generations gather for the sixtieth wedding anniversary of Emma and Moses Chandler (seated in front), parents of Harry Chandler. This photo was taken on August 27, 1922, three days before the wedding of Harry's son Norman (standing farthest right) to Dorothy Buffum. Only one of Norman's six siblings attended the wedding. It was the first public display of a Chandler family divide.

Van Nuys, Isaac, 86

Vietnam War, 141, 157, 166, 195

Wall Street Journal, 162, 163, 196, 197

Warren, Earl, 94, 95, 106, 151

Washington Post, 168

Watergate scandal, 124

Watts Riots, 90, 116, 130, 156, 157

Waxman, Al, 117

Weeks, Paul, 120, 154

Wetherby, Eliza, 19

Whitaker, Bettina, 165, 180

White, Stephen Mallory, 32

Wiggins, Frank, 28

Willes, Mark, 195, 197

Williams, Nick, 122, 149, 151, 152

Williamson, Tad, 125, 179

World War I, 8, 72, 74, 81, 83, 90, 113, 114, 115

World War II, 8, 81, 83, 113, 114, 115

Zoot Suit Riot, 115, 116, 117, 118, 120

Inventing L.A.: The Chandlers and Their Times
by Bill Boyarsky / based on the film by Peter Jones

Copyright © 2009 by Bill Boyarsky and Peter Jones

10 9 8 7 6 5 4 3 2 1
ISBN-13 978 1-883318-92-5

Design: Amy Inouye, futurestudio.com
Photo Editor: Mark Catalena
Photo Curator: Brian Tessier

LIBRARY OF CONGRESS CATALOGING-IN-PUBLICATION DATA

Boyarsky, Bill.
 Inventing L.A. : the Chandlers and their Times / by Bill Boyarsky ; based on the film by Peter Jones.
    p. cm.
 Summary: "Inventing L.A.: The Chandlers and Their Times" is the tale of the Chandlers family's reign over L.A. with the help of their mighty scepter, the Times, and their entwinement with politics, family feud, and fortune. This is truly the story of the building of one of the most famous, populated, and culturally rich cities in the world"—Provided by publisher.
 Includes bibliographical references and index.
 ISBN 978-1-883318-92-5 (hardcover : alk. paper)
 1. Los Angeles times. 2. Otis, Harrison Gray, 1837-1917. 3. Chandler, Harry, 1864-1944. 4. Chandler, Norman, b. 1899. 5. Chandler, Otis, 1927-2006. 6. Newspaper publishing—California—Los Angeles. I. Jones, Peter, 1956 Feb. 24- II. Title.
 PN4899.L64.L6622 2009
 070.5'7220979494—dc22

                        2009027948

ANGEL CITY PRESS
2118 Wilshire Blvd. #880
Santa Monica, California 90403
310.395.9982
www.angelcitypress.com

This book is a companion to the film Inventing L.A.: The Chandlers and Their Times, which was made possible in part by funding from The Annenberg Foundation, The Charles B. Thornton Family, The California Council for the Humanities' California Stories Initiative, The Skirball Foundation, The David Bohnett Foundation, and PBS.